DATE DUE			

PRESIDENTS
and their
DECISIONS

GEORGE
W. BUSH

Book Editors:

TOM LANSFORD, PhD
UNIVERSITY OF SOUTHERN MISSISSIPPI

ROBERT P. WATSON, PhD
FLORIDA ATLANTIC UNIVERSITY

BRUCE GLASSMAN, *Vice Publisher*
BONNIE SZUMSKI, *Publisher*
HELEN COTHRAN, *Managing Editor*

GREENHAVEN PRESS
An imprint of Thomson Gale, a part of The Thomson Corporation

THOMSON
━━━✦━━━
GALE

etroit • New York • San Francisco • San Diego • New Haven, Conn.
Waterville, Maine • London • Munich

LIBRARY OF CONGRESS CATALOGING-IN-PUBLICATION DATA

George W. Bush / Tom Lansford and Robert P. Watson, book editors.
   p. cm. — (Presidents and their decisions)
   Includes bibliographical references and index.
   ISBN 0-7377-2597-4 (alk. paper)
     1. Bush, George W. (George Walker), 1946– . 2. United States—Politics and government—2001—Decision making. 3. United States—Foreign relations—2001—Decision making. I. Lansford, Tom. II. Watson, Robert P., 1962– .
III. Series.
   E902.G45 2005
   973.931'092—dc22
                                                      2004052351

Printed in the United States of America

CONTENTS

CHAPTER 3: THE ECONOMY

FOREWORD

"**T**HE PRESIDENCY OF THE UNITED STATES IS OFTEN DE-scribed as the most powerful office in the world," writes Forrest McDonald in *The American Presidency: An Intellectual History*. "In one sense this description is accurate," he says, "for even casual decisions made in the White House can affect the lives of millions of people." But McDonald also notes that presidential power "is restrained by the countervailing power of Congress, the courts, the bureaucracy, popular opinion, the news media, and state and local governments. What presidents do have is awesome responsibilities combined with unique opportunities to persuade others to do their bidding—opportunities enhanced by the possibility of dispensing favors, by the mystique of presidential power, and by the aura of monarchy that surrounds the president."

The way various presidents have used the complex power of their office is the subject of Greenhaven Press's Presidents and Their Decisions series. Each volume in the series examines one particular president and the key decisions he made while in office.

Some presidential decisions have been made in a relatively brief period of time, as with Abraham Lincoln's suspension of the writ of habeus corpus at the start of the Civil War. Others were refined as they were implemented over a period of years, as was the case with Franklin Delano Roosevelt's struggle to lead the country out of the Great Depression. Some presidential actions are generally lauded by historians—for example, Lyndon Johnson's support of the civil rights movement in the 1960s—while others have been condemned—such as Richard Nixon's ef-

7

forts, from 1972 to 1974, to cover up the involvement of his aides in the Watergate scandal.

Most of the truly history-making presidential decisions, though, remain the subject of intense scrutiny and historical debate. Many of these were made during a time of war or other crisis, in which a president was forced to risk either spectacular success or devastating failure. Examples include Lincoln's much-scrutinized handling of the crisis at Fort Sumter, the first conflict of the Civil War; FDR's efforts to aid the European Allies at the beginning of World War II; Harry Truman's controversial decision to use the atomic bomb in order to end that conflict; and Lyndon Johnson's fateful decision to escalate the war in Vietnam.

Each volume in the Presidents and Their Decisions series devotes a full chapter to each of the president's key decisions. The essays in each chapter, most written by presidential historians and biographers, offer a range of perspectives on the president and his actions. Some provide background on the political, social, and economic factors behind a particular decision. Others critique the president's performance, offering a negative or positive appraisal. Essays have been chosen for their concise and engaging presentation of the facts, and each is preceded by a straightforward summary of the article's content.

In addition to the articles, these books include extensive material to help the student researcher. An opening essay provides both a brief biography of the president and an overview of the events that occurred during his time in office. A chronology also helps readers keep track of the dates of specific events. A comprehensive index and an annotated table of contents aid readers in quickly locating material of interest, and an extensive bibliography serves as a launching point for further research. Finally, an appendix of primary historical documents provides a sampling of the president's most important speeches, as well as some of his contemporaries' criticisms.

Greenhaven Press's Presidents and Their Decisions series will help students gain a deeper understanding of the decisions made by some of the most influential leaders in American history.

George W. Bush: A Biography

AT 9:00 A.M. ON SEPTEMBER 11, 2001, AS HE ENTERED AN elementary school in Sarasota, Florida, President George W. Bush was informed that an airplane had crashed into one of the twin towers of the World Trade Center (WTC) in New York City. A few minutes later, as Bush sat reading to a second-grade class, his chief of staff, Andrew Card, whispered to him that a second plane had struck the other WTC tower. Card then uttered the startling statement, "America is under attack."[1] Unsure of the true extent of the attacks, Bush left the school. He then spoke by phone with his national security adviser, Condoleezza Rice, who said that two other airliners seemed to have been hijacked as well. Thus began what would be one of the most extraordinary periods in the history of the American presidency.

By the end of the day on September 11, a third passenger jet had crashed into the Pentagon while a fourth hijacked airliner went down in western Pennsylvania after its passengers apparently rose up against their hijackers. The attacks destroyed the twin towers of the WTC and left more than three thousand Americans and citizens of other nations dead, with thousands more injured. The attacks caused widespread economic and social disruption and prompted the Bush administration to initiate a global "war on terror." The result was a recalculation of both domestic and international security programs. The attacks also marked a dramatic change in U.S. foreign policy. Like the administrations of his predecessors William McKinley and Franklin D. Roosevelt, Bush's presidency came to be defined by attacks on the United States even as the nation also grappled with a range of contentious domestic issues.

Early Life

George W. Bush's parents, Barbara P. and George Herbert Walker Bush, came from privileged New York families. She was the daughter of a publishing mogul and he the son of an investment banker who later served as a Republican senator from Connecticut. The two were married in 1945 after George H.W. Bush returned from his service in World War II. The couple's first son, George Walker Bush, was born on July 6, 1946, in New Haven, Connecticut, where the senior Bush was finishing his degree at Yale. Determined to break away from the influence of their families and to make their own way in the world, the Bushes left New England in 1948 for Odessa, Texas, where George W. Bush's father started a career in the oil business. The elder Bush eventually founded his own oil company and became wealthy in his own right, selling his company for $1 million in 1966.

The family lived in an upper-middle-class neighborhood in Midland, Texas. The father worked tirelessly in the oilfields, and it fell to Barbara Bush to raise the children and run the household. After George H.W. Bush sold his oil company, he embarked on a career in politics, which also caused him to be absent for lengthy periods. This absence further contributed to Barbara's serving as the essential head of the household. Many people who knew the Bushes during this period often remark that George, as the oldest son, often functioned as the "man of the house" in his father's absence. When Barbara suffered a miscarriage, it was her son who drove her to the hospital since the elder Bush was out of town.

As a child, George W. Bush emerged as a natural leader. He also clearly loved being the center of attention. As a youth, he played football and baseball and became his class president while in junior high school. The Bushes eventually had five other children: three sons, Jeb, Neil, and Marvin; and two daughters, Pauline (or "Robin") and Dorothy. Pauline Robinson Bush died of leukemia in October 1953. Robin's death profoundly affected the young family. Bush later described the tragedy as "the starkest memory of my childhood, a sharp pain in the midst of an otherwise happy blur."[2]

After the family moved to Houston, Bush was enrolled at a private school. In 1961, the Bushes decided to send George to the prestigious Philips Academy, which his father had attended, in Andover, Massachusetts. The move from Texas to Massachusetts was traumatic for Bush. Not only did he experience culture shock, but he found himself competing with the legacy of his father, who had been senior class president and captain of the baseball team. At Andover, his academic performance was a disappointment to his parents as he managed only average grades, struggling with his school work and often lacking discipline. Bush would later confide to friends that he was often afraid he would fail out of Andover. He did excel at athletics, however, playing both baseball and basketball, and was popular with his fellow students.

Bush entered Yale University in 1964. There he had an undistinguished academic record but was popular socially. He was admitted to the secretive Skull and Bones organization and became president of his fraternity, Delta Kappa Epsilon. Bush also became a heavy social drinker and spent considerable time partying.

His Own Man

To a large extent, Bush's early life was lived in the footsteps of his father. During the two decades after his graduation from Yale, Bush continued to compete with his father's legacy even as he endeavored to become his own man. And what a legacy it was: The elder Bush had served in Congress from 1966 to 1970. He was then appointed ambassador to the United Nations (UN) and a special envoy to China. In 1975, he became chairman of the Republican National Party, and he served as director of the Central Intelligence Agency from 1975 to 1977.

During the late 1960s and early 1970s, the younger Bush worked on several of his father's political races and Senate campaigns in Alabama and Florida. In doing so, he developed a reputation within the Republican Party in Texas as a competent campaigner, but he did not seem especially interested in pursuing a political career.

Instead, as his graduation from Yale neared, Bush applied for admission to law school at the University of Texas but was denied admission. Two weeks before graduation in 1968, Bush joined the Texas Air National Guard, where he trained as a fighter pilot. His tenure in the National Guard allowed him to avoid service in Vietnam, and he was honorably discharged in 1973. Unable to go to the law school of his choice, Bush instead decided to pursue a master of business administration degree (MBA) at Harvard. He completed the program in 1975 and returned to Texas to start a career in the oil business. In spite of his Harvard credentials, Bush took an entry-level job in land acquisitions.

In 1977 friends arranged for Bush to meet Laura Welch at a backyard cookout. The two had been classmates in grade school, but while Bush had gone to the Northeast for his education, Laura had remained in Texas, where she attended Southern Methodist University and the University of Texas, then worked as a teacher and school librarian. The extroverted, boisterous Bush seemed a strange match for the quiet, introverted Welch, but the two quickly fell in love and were married on November 5, 1977, only three months after they met.

At about this time, Bush attempted to embark on a new career path—elected office. In 1978, Bush's political ambitions suddenly surfaced when he unexpectedly announced a run for the U.S. House of Representatives. He defeated a well-known and well-financed opponent in the Republican primary, but was defeated in the general election. Still, Bush received 47 percent of the vote in a district that had never elected a Republican. Bush then worked on his father's presidential campaign in 1980. When the senior Bush became vice president to Ronald Reagan, the junior Bush decided that he could not run for political office until his father retired from politics. He therefore refocused his energies on the oil business.

After his failed congressional campaign, Bush founded an oil exploration company, Arbusto Energy (*arbusto* is Spanish for "bush"). The late 1970s were a boom time for oil companies, and Bush initially did quite well. Over a three-year period, Arbusto attracted $3 million in investments. After Laura Bush delivered twin girls, Barbara and Jenna (named after their grandmothers) in 1981, the family sought to gain financial independence. However, the pressure to provide for his family was not enough to stop Bush's drinking, and he continued to drink heavily even after the birth of the twins and as he began to enjoy financial success.

The year 1986 marked a major turning point in Bush's life. After a raucous party to celebrate his fortieth birthday, Bush awoke with a massive hangover and the realization that his frequent binge drinking was harming his relationship with his family and his career. He became determined to stop drinking entirely, a decision that would evolve into a spiritual awakening and a commitment to Christianity. His newfound faith, which was inspired by an earlier meeting with the Reverend Billy Graham, led Bush to become increasingly active in the church through service such as Sunday school and Bible study.[3]

Bush became a political consultant for his father's presidential campaign in 1988. After his father won the election, Bush led an investment group that purchased a share of the Texas Rangers professional baseball team. His family name and connections helped draw together a well-financed offer, and the group successfully acquired an 86 percent stake in the team. Bush became the public head of the franchise, but the actual business operations were overseen by Edward "Rusty" Rose. Bush and Rose were able to gain backing for a new stadium and thereby substantially increased the value of the team. Revenues increased from $28 million a year to $62 million within a year and subsequently continued to grow. The position secured Bush's status as a public figure. His ability to secure voter approval for a public financing deal for the new stadium convinced many in the state Republican Party that Bush would make a viable and formidable candidate for high public office. In 1990, a number of influential Texans approached Bush about running for governor, but Bush declined because he did not want his political activities to affect his father's presidency.[4]

In the meantime, Bush returned to Washington to help with his father's 1992 reelection campaign. He was named a senior adviser for the campaign and participated in both the behind-the-scenes strategy development and the public campaign events such as speeches.[5] The campaign increased Bush's visibility and enhanced his political credentials nationally and among party insiders. However, by October the polls clearly indicated that his father was losing, which the younger Bush also realized weeks before the vote.[6] George H.W. Bush lost the 1992 election to Bill Clinton. Bush was deeply disappointed with the outcome of the election, but with his father out of the political limelight, the younger Bush was free to try again to launch his own political career.

Governor of Texas

Even before his father left office and Bill Clinton was sworn in, Republicans in Texas began a lobbying effort to convince Bush to run for the governorship. The Democratic incumbent, Ann Richards, was barely halfway through her first term, but many Republicans thought she was vulnerable, especially in light of a school funding crisis in the state. The growing success of the Rangers baseball franchise had not only increased Bush's popularity and financial security, but provided a possible contrast with Governor Richards, who was dealing with a tight state budget.

Bush was enthusiastic about running for office, but his wife was initially reluctant. Her hesitation, however, was soon overcome by Bush's enthusiasm.

As he began to build his campaign team, Bush avoided using people with connections to his father and tried to ensure that his campaign would be perceived as "home-grown" by Texans, who might otherwise question the roots of a Yankee transplant. He chose Karl Rove to be one of his main advisers. Rove would go on to work on both of Bush's gubernatorial campaigns and his two presidential bids. Bush eventually settled on Joe Allbaugh as his campaign manager; like Rove, Allbaugh would also serve in Bush's later campaigns. Rove arranged a series of meetings between Bush and senior Republicans around the state and began to develop an effective fund-raising machine.

The 1994 campaign began with the two candidates in a virtual dead heat according to polls, but Bush was able to steadily gain the advantage over Richards. Bush proved to be an unflappable candidate who refused to be drawn into a negative campaign when his opponent ran hostile advertising. Bush won the upset election 53 percent to 46 percent. His main support came from white males, but he also surprised the experts by receiving greater than expected support from women and Hispanic voters.

After the election, Bush removed himself from the daily operations of the Rangers. The team was eventually purchased for $250 million, of which Bush received $14.9 million, a handsome profit and huge increase on his small initial investment. As governor, Bush developed a reputation for bipartisanship. He worked closely with the Democratic lieutenant governor, Bob Bullock, and was able to secure passage of most of his legislative agenda even though the legislature was initially controlled by the Democratic Party. In his first year, Bush presided over a wide-ranging series of tort reforms designed to limit lawsuit awards and thereby control insurance costs for businesses and the medical industry. Bush also proposed a series of measures that increased punishments for juvenile offenders and expanded juvenile detention centers. In 1997 the Texas legislature enacted health maintenance organization (HMO) reforms. Bush opposed several components of the original plan but was able to craft compromises with the aid of Lieutenant Governor Bullock. These various legislative packages proved very popular with the public.

Bush easily won reelection in 1998 with more than 68 percent of the vote. He became the first gubernatorial incumbent in Texas to be elected to consecutive terms in the twentieth century. Because of Bush's popularity, Republicans also captured the main state offices, including those of the lieutenant governor, attorney general, comptroller, and commissioner of agriculture. The year 1998 also brought another electoral victory for the Bush family, as George's brother Jeb was elected governor of Florida. In the aftermath of the election, speculation began about George W. Bush running for the presidency in 2000.

As he began his second term, Bush sought to capitalize on his popularity to enact educational reforms and to promote faith-based social initiatives. He also began organizing a presidential campaign. Republicans were eager to end eight years of Democratic control of the White House. As a result, Bush took an early lead in fund-raising. By the time of the election, Bush had raised an astonishing $193 million compared to the $132 million raised by his opponent, Democratic incumbent vice president Al Gore.

The 2000 Election Controversy

Bush began the campaign with a commanding lead in the polls, but as the election neared, Gore was able to close the gap and make the election one of the closest and most controversial in American history.[7] On the evening of the election (November 7, 2000), the race appeared to come down to one state: Florida. At roughly 7:30 P.M. (EST), the television networks declared Al Gore the winner of Florida, which essentially meant he had won the presidency. But this announcement proved premature, because the polls had not closed and initial results from Florida were inaccurate. A mere two-and-one-half hours later, the same networks were forced to retract their announcement.[8] As midnight passed, the election was too close to call, with only 1,768 votes separating the two candidates. Across the country, the public went to bed not knowing who had won the election. Al Gore, after initially celebrating, then conceding defeat, withdrew his concession and called for a recount of the votes in Florida.

In the days following the election, numerous allegations highlighting irregularities in Florida's vote put into question the reliability of the election.[9] Attempts to recount the disputed votes resulted in small changes to Bush's narrow lead, which, when a manual recount concluded on November 15, stood at a mere 327 votes. However, as the due date for declaring a victor loomed, the U.S. Supreme Court ruled in a controversial 5-4 split vote in favor of Bush, stopping the recount process and essentially declaring Bush the winner.[10] Critics alleged Republican partisanship by the high court, foul play by Florida's elections director, Katherine Harris, and incompetence by elections officials. To make matters worse, Al Gore had actually received half a million more popular votes nationwide than George W. Bush. However, it is not the popular vote that elects the president, but the Electoral College. To be successful, a candidate must receive a majority (more than 270) of the Electoral College votes. With Florida in his column, Bush attained the magic number by a single vote and became the forty-third president of the United States.

Transition to Power and First Hundred Days

The controversies surrounding Bush's election not only delayed the time available for an already short and tenuous transition from campaigning to governing, but presented challenges unique to a president whose very credibility was in question. The president-elect has only a short ten weeks from the time of the election to the inauguration during which to screen and select dozens of top aides and cabinet officers. During this time and in the initial months of the new administration, the president must also make thousands of appointments to fill the senior administrative posts in government. Many of these appointments must be confirmed by the Senate. In addition to gaining Senate support for the administration's nominees, the president must also consider the special skills needed by each appointee, the need to achieve geographic and ethnic diversity in staffing, and the loyalty of the new appointees.

The challenge Bush faced in overcoming an abbreviated transition because of the contested election was formidable. As James P. Pfiffner has noted, presidents must "hit the ground running"[11] because the "honeymoon" period usually afforded new presidents rarely lasts more than one hundred days before their limited "political capital" begins to erode. This time period also offers an opportunity to establish the White House's agenda and develop a positive rapport with media and public. Recognizing the limited time available, and the need to be able take immediate action, Bush's vice president-elect, Dick Cheney, who had been through such transitions as a former presidential adviser, wisely suggested establishing a transition office while the election outcome was still pending.

Bush selected high-profile, popular individuals such as Colin Powell—his secretary of state designee—early in the process, ensuring Senate confirmation and guaranteeing he would have his senior staff in place at the start of his term. Indeed, on January 20, 2005, the day of the inauguration, the Senate confirmed seven—fully half—of Bush's cabinet nominees, including Powell. Within weeks, Bush had much of his team in place. For many Americans, the efficiency and effectiveness of the Bush transition and initial staffing overshadowed the credibility problem caused by the election controversy.[12] Bush selected seasoned veterans of the White House, producing one of the most experienced administrations in recent times and generally earning widespread praise from scholars and the media.[13] The Bush team was also surprisingly diverse for a Republican administration. The cabinet contained four women, two African Americans, one Hispanic, and two Asian Americans.

Bush enjoyed an impressively smooth transition. His team did not mishandle any appointments and had success in getting the nominees confirmed in the Senate. The only nominee who failed to win confirmation was Linda Chavez, the labor secretary designee, who was forced to withdraw her nomination because she may have violated federal laws in hiring an illegal immigrant maid. Chavez was a polarizing figure who failed to disclose the information about hiring the illegal immigrant although she had been vocal in her criticism of others for similar missteps. Although Bush's choice for attorney general, John Ashcroft, was confirmed, his nomination resulted in a bitter partisan feud in the Senate, one that spilled over into the press. Indeed, Bush's picks were noteworthy not only for being highly experienced and generally well regarded: They established the Bush administration as one of the most ideologically conservative and highly partisan in the history of the office.

Presidential Agenda

Perhaps the most impressive political success—and clearly the most surprising—of the Bush presidency was the Republican victory in the midterm elections of 2002. The political party of a sitting president usually does poorly in midterm elections (elections when the president is not up for reelection). Expectations were therefore low for the Republicans in 2002, and conventional wisdom suggested that

Bush would invest little political capital in the races in order to avoid the political embarrassment of campaigning for, but losing, congressional seats. But even with history against him, the president actively campaigned for his party and numerous Republican candidates. Bush and his aides succeeded in nationalizing the election by emphasizing his character and bold leadership of the war against terrorism rather than policy matters in particular congressional districts and states. Bush gambled but won big. Republicans actually gained seats in Congress, which had happened only twice since the Civil War. The campaign showed that Bush had the support of the nation.[14] The victories also gave the Republicans a majority in both houses of Congress and gave Bush the mandate to push his agenda that he lacked after the controversial 2000 election that brought him into office.

The Bush agenda included as a centerpiece the president's campaign pledge to cut taxes. The unprecedented economic growth the nation had enjoyed in the mid- and late 1990s had slowed by the time Bush entered office; by the time of the terrorist attacks on September 11, 2001, the economy was teetering on recession. As a capitalist, George W. Bush was a fervent believer in the free market. He thought that, just as government programs were not the solution to socioeconomic problems, the economy was better served by less government intervention or management. The president therefore believed that large tax cuts would boost the ailing economy and stem the loss of jobs. He packaged his proposed $1.6 trillion tax cuts with an eye to politics by framing the amount as too much for liberals and too little for conservatives. The public debate never really considered *whether* tax cuts were necessary, but rather focused on the amount. Bush said that he was simply giving the people's money back to them ("the surplus is not the government's money"[15]) and that having more money in everyone's pocket would boost spending, which would boost the economy. This simple rhetoric pleased the public while, behind the scenes, Bush built bipartisan support for his proposal. In the end, he agreed to trim the figure a little, which gave the impression that this was a president willing to compromise but one who fulfilled his campaign promises. The record tax cuts were enacted and Bush scored an impressive political victory.

Critics claimed that the country had gone from a record budget surplus to ballooning, record deficits in the short time of Bush's watch and alleged that the tax cuts were a giveaway that disproportionately benefited the wealthy. By the time of Bush's reelection effort in 2004, the economic signals were mixed: The president pointed to some signs that the economy was recovering, but Democrats noted that Bush would be the first president since Herbert Hoover to have a net loss of jobs during his administration.

In addition to tax cuts, Bush's domestic agenda included education reform. The core element of Bush's education plan was the establishment of standardized testing to assess the performance of schools, teachers, and students and to hold them accountable for the results.

An assortment of other issues and proposals rounded out Bush's agenda. These included military preparedness in the aftermath of the September 11 attacks. The president pushed for increases in military spending, overturned the ban on nuclear weapons testing, and advocated reintroducing the missile defense system. Bush also embraced faith-based initiatives, which meant giving government funds to religious organizations that provided social services. In addition, Bush promoted a new energy policy based on increased oil drilling and exploration.

While Bush was successful in securing legislation to support his tax, education, military, and faith-based initiatives, his energy and environmental policies proved far more controversial and evoked considerable congressional opposition. For instance, the Senate repeatedly blocked Bush's efforts to open the Arctic National Wildlife Refuge in Alaska for new oil drilling. In addition, public opposition prevented the administration from increasing the amount of arsenic allowed in drinking water. Bush also was criticized for his decision to withdraw U.S. support for the Kyoto Protocol, an international treaty designed to prevent global warming.

New Directions in Foreign Policy

During his campaign for the presidency, George W. Bush had made several public gaffes when commenting on international relations, which reinforced his image as someone who was neither interested nor well versed in the intricacies of foreign policy. For instance, despite his family's wealth and extensive service in national politics—including his father's stints as U.S. ambassador to the United Nations and envoy to China—George W. Bush had hardly traveled internationally and did not know the names of world leaders when asked. Early in his presidency, during unscripted remarks on U.S.-Taiwan relations, Bush highlighted his inexperience by commenting that the United States had an obligation to defend Taiwan from China, even if military force was required. The comment, which stood in contrast to decades of stated U.S. policy, heightened tensions with China. Bush also unilaterally withdrew the United States from many international treaties, threatened trading partners with tariffs and other protectionist measures, placed a low priority on the Middle East peace process, and repeatedly made public pronouncements against the United Nations. As a result, many allies felt alienated or offended by U.S. policies, and Bush gained the image internationally as a "Lone Ranger" unilateralist.

All that changed on September 11, 2001. In two days following the terrorist attacks on America, Bush's approval rating in the polls went from an unspectacular 50 percent to roughly 90 percent. Not only did the president gain an impressive jump in public support as the nation rallied behind its leader and the flag, but over the ensuing months he was able to sustain high approval ratings. In fact, for a two-year period after the attacks Bush enjoyed the highest average approval ratings of any president since such polls have been taken.[16]

Emerging from the rubble of September 11 transformed into a strong war president and patriot, Bush successfully rallied the American public to support a new and difficult global war against terror. From his appearances standing atop the rubble at the former site of the World Trade Center, to his visits with the troops, to his appeals for public prayer, Bush generally received widespread support from the public, press, and Congress. Internationally, the September 11 tragedy occasioned a sense of solidarity between the United States and the world community. For the first time in its half-century history, the North Atlantic Treaty Organization invoked Article 5 of its charter, which declared that an attack on one member was an attack on all members. A leading French newspaper proclaimed in bold headlines, "We are all Americans." And Palestinian leader Yasir Arafat even donated blood in a symbolic gesture of healing.

George W. Bush was never considered a great speaker, but he found a voice and cause after the terrorist attacks. Bush's aggressive, quick response to the terrorist strikes not only launched a new global war against terrorism but marked a fundamental change in the nature and conduct of American foreign policy. Bush defined the effort as a global war against the foremost threat to national security, rather than as a law enforcement issue. The American response was a war on all fronts to be fought by securing national borders, freezing financial assets used by terrorists, and taking military action against terrorists and nations supporting terrorists. Within weeks of the attacks, the United States invaded Afghanistan and quickly and efficiently destroyed the repressive Taliban regime that had harbored the September 11 mastermind Osama bin Laden.

A centerpiece of the war on the domestic front was the establishment of the Department of Homeland Security (DHS), which constituted the most sweeping restructuring of the federal government since the administration of Franklin Roosevelt. Although Bush initially opposed both the creation of DHS and the federalization of airport security, he ultimately embraced the ideas once it became clear that they were popular with the public. The new super-agency consolidated the many units of the federal government responsible for the country's borders, harbors, immigration, emergency management response, and protection. Bush and the new agency received credit for averting subsequent terrorist attacks in the critical months after the September 11 hijackings.[17]

Despite the successful war against Afghanistan, the president's detractors claimed that the DHS and the conduct of the antiterrorist campaign—using military tribunals, wiretapping, expanding search and seizure and arrest powers, and reducing media and public access to government—infringed on civil liberties. A range of citizen groups, including the American Civil Liberties Union, undertook various legal challenges to many of Bush's policies. However, the courts granted wide latitude for the administration to expand the federal government's surveillance and detainment powers. One exception was a June 2004 Supreme Court ruling that denied the government the right to detain "enemy combatants" indefinitely without trial.

The Bush Doctrine and Iraq

In his 2002 State of the Union address, Bush declared that Iran, Iraq, and North Korea constituted an "axis of evil" that threatened the "peace of the world" because of their support for international terrorism and their pursuit of weapons of mass destruction (WMDs).[18] Bush pledged that he would not risk the safety and security of the United States in the face of threats to national security and would launch preemptive attacks to protect the nation. This preemptive doctrine was codified in the 2002 National Security Strategy, which declared that the United States would strike first in order to prevent WMD attacks or catastrophic terrorist events such as the September 11 attacks. This strategy of preemptive war became known as the Bush Doctrine. It proved very controversial in the United States and abroad as scholars and politicians debated whether preemptive attacks were legal under international law. While international law allows states to launch preemptive attacks when imminently threatened by other nations, what constitutes an "imminent threat" remains difficult to define and hotly contested.

The first application of the Bush Doctrine was the invasion of Iraq. Iraqi dictator Saddam Hussein had defied international laws for many years and had failed to comply fully with weapons inspections required in the wake of the Persian Gulf War in 1991. President Bush warned Hussein to comply with weapons inspectors and alleged that the Iraqi strongman was both complicit in the September 11 terrorist attacks and guilty of stockpiling WMDs. Bush initially gained multilateral support, including a unanimous UN Security Council resolution, for renewed WMD inspections. During a period of intense diplomatic activity in the fall of 2002, the Bush administration tried to develop a coalition of nations to support an invasion and the removal of Hussein, while other countries sought a nonmilitary resolution to the issue.

The Bush administration gained the support of Australia, Japan, and about half of the European countries, including the United Kingdom, Spain, Italy, and all of the eastern European states. But France, Germany, Belgium, and other major world powers, such as Russia and China, opposed military action. These countries argued that UN weapons inspectors were making progress and only needed more time. In addition, even within the countries that officially supported the war, public opinion often ran counter to that of the government. However, long-standing historical ties and the importance of friendship with the United States led many states to back the Bush administration. A succession of reports from the weapons inspectors only clouded matters by noting progress but also ongoing efforts by Hussein's regime to deceive the inspectors and avoid full cooperation. Efforts to gain a second UN resolution to authorize the use of force failed, and Bush decided to invade Iraq with a small coalition of willing countries. On March 20, 2003, Bush took the war on terror to Iraq. American forces quickly routed the Iraqi army and, by April 14, Hussein's regime had been toppled. Hussein was captured by American forces in December 2003.

Winning the peace has proved more difficult than defeating the armies of Afghanistan and Iraq. In Iraq as well as in the wider Arab world, American forces were often seen as occupiers rather than liberators. American credibility has been further undermined because the WMDs cited by Bush as a major reason for going to war were not found by international weapons inspectors, and the evidence linking Hussein and Iraq to the September 11 attacks proved inaccurate. Also, despite Hussein's removal, the ongoing occupation of Iraq has proved difficult, and more U.S. troops were killed in vigilante attacks after the major combat operations than during the actual war. Bush has been criticized for poor postwar planning. Many argue that Osama bin Laden and his terrorist organization al Qaeda were the real enemies and that the war in Iraq was a costly distraction that only further inflamed anti-American sentiment. Critics at home and abroad have accused Bush of arrogance and reckless warmongering. Internationally, the unprecedented goodwill shown toward the United States in the aftermath of September 11 had, by 2004, eroded to the point where close allies openly opposed U.S. policies, and anti-American sentiment was at an all-time high around the globe.

Conclusion

Throughout his political career, George W. Bush has benefited from low expectations. His opponents often made the
mistake of underestimating him, a mistake that more often
than not proved costly for them. So too have the reduced
public expectations of his performance permitted him to
frequently exceed expectations. Bush also benefited from
the scandals and perceived character deficiencies of his
predecessor, Bill Clinton. Clinton's failings allowed Bush to
cast himself as a strong and truthful leader, one who returned character and integrity to the White House. The
Bush record, not surprisingly and like that of all presidents, can be seen as mixed.

The president has enjoyed considerable public support
at home, while attracting disdain internationally. His supporters claim that he has delivered on his campaign pledges
to be a "compassionate conservative" who is "a uniter, not a
divider." His opponents say otherwise. Either way, George
W. Bush has transformed American foreign policy and has
led a new type of war against a new type of enemy. The final
chapters of the wars in Afghanistan and Iraq, and the larger war against terror, have not yet been written. How history will judge President George W. Bush remains to be seen.

Notes

1. Christopher Anderson, *George and Laura: Portrait of an American Marriage.* New York: William Morrow, 2002, p. 3.
2. George W. Bush, *A Charge to Keep: My Journey to the White House.* New York: William Morrow, 1999; reprint, New York: Harper-Collins, 2001, p. 14.
3. Bush and Hughes, *A Charge to Keep,* pp. 136–38. See also Stephen Mansfield, *The Faith of George W. Bush.* Los Angeles: J.P. Tarcher Press, 2003.
4. Bill Minutaglio, *First Son: George W. Bush and the Bush Family Dynasty.* New York: Times Books, 1999, p. 265.
5. Herbert Parmet, *George Bush: The Life of a Lonestar Yankee.* New

York: Scribner's, 1997; reprint, New Brunswick, NJ: Transaction, 2001, p. 302.

6. Mary Matlin and James Carville, *All's Fair: Love, War and Running for President.* New York: Random House, 1994, p. 452.

7. James W. Ceaser and Andrew E. Busch, *The Perfect Tie: The True Story of the 2000 Presidential Election.* Lanham, MD: Rowman & Littlefield, 2001, p. 1.

8. Ceaser and Busch, *The Perfect Tie,* pp. 8–10.

9. For a detailed examination of the events surrounding the election, see Robert P. Watson, ed., *Counting Votes: Lessons Learned from the 2000 Presidential Election in Florida.* Gainesville: University Press of Florida, 2004.

10. For a detailed discussion of the legal issues and court cases surrounding the Bush-Gore election controversy, see E.J. Dionne and William Kristol, *Bush v. Gore: The Court Cases and the Commentary.* Washington, DC: Brookings Institution Press, 2001.

11. James P. Pfiffner, *The Strategic Presidency: Hitting the Ground Running.* 2nd ed. Lawrence: University Press of Kansas, 1996, p. 6.

12. Joseph A. Pika, John Anthony Maltese, and Norman C. Thomas, *The Politics of the Presidency.* 5th ed. Washington, DC: CQ Press, 2002, p. 401.

13. Bradley H. Patteson Jr., "The New Bush White House: Choices Being Made," *White House Studies,* vol. 1, no. 2, 2001, pp. 225–36.

14. Gary C. Jacobson and Samuel Kernell, *The Logic of American Politics in Wartime: Lessons from the Bush Administration.* Washington, DC: CQ Press, 2004, pp. 7–9.

15. George W. Bush, address at the White House, June 7, 2001.

16. For an examination of Bush's approval ratings and his foreign policy, see Bryan Hilliard, Tom Lansford, and Robert P. Watson, eds., *George W. Bush: Evaluating the President at Midterm.* Albany, NY: SUNY Press, 2004.

17. Gary L. Gregg II, "Dignified Authenticity: George W. Bush and the Symbolic Presidency," in Gary L. Gregg II and Mark J. Rozell, eds., *Considering the Bush Presidency.* New York: Oxford University Press, 2004, pp. 93–105.

18. George W. Bush, State of the Union address, January 29, 2002.

CHAPTER

1

THE WAR
ON TERROR

Bush's Response to the September 11 Attacks Enhanced His Credibility

Stanley A. Renshon

Few events have had as dramatic an impact on a presidency as the terrorist attacks of September 11, 2001. The attacks severely tested the leadership abilities of George W. Bush. Polls conducted immediately after the attacks indicated that most Americans approved of Bush's initial actions in the war on terror, including his strong show of patriotism and his emphasis on national security. This was in direct contrast to views of him prior to the attacks; indeed, many saw him as weak and stiff. According to Stanley A. Renshon in the following selection, Bush's strong patriotic and independent stance after the attacks illustrated an inner confidence and focus that had been invisible before. Renshon is a professor of political science at City University of New York Graduate Center and the author of numerous books on the presidency.

THE ANSWER TO THE QUESTION OF WHETHER THE BUSH presidency has been transformed as a result of 9/11 is clear. It has. The question of whether Bush himself has been transformed is more complex. Certainly, a president's

Stanley A. Renshon, "The World According to George W. Bush," *Good Judgment in Foreign Policy: Theory and Application*, edited by Stanley A. Renshon and Deborah Welch Larson. New York: Rowman & Littlefield Publishers, 2003. Copyright © 2003 by Rowman & Littlefield Publishers, Inc. All rights reserved. Reproduced by permission.

response to dramatic and extremely critical events gives us a measure of the man and his leadership. It is also true that presidential responses to even momentous events must begin with the basic building blocks and raw materials of a president's psychology, character and leadership skills.

Karl Rove, Bush's senior adviser, was asked about this:

> Thomas Mann: Karl, to the outside world, it looks as if there have been two George W. Bush presidencies already, the pre–September 11 and the post–September 11. Is that simply a caricature of what we see?

> Rove: Well, I'm not certain it is that much different. . . . I for one don't buy this theory that September 11th somehow changed George W. Bush. . . . But really since September 11th, I think what America has seen—and great events do not transform presidents. They bring out who they are. . . . So my view is that all this about he's changed and he's transformed, no, he's who he is, required to do more in a great crisis, so you don't manufacture these things. You don't create them. They're either there or they're not. The moment calls them out or the moment doesn't. The moment requires something of you, and you're either able to do or you aren't.

Gravitas?

Rove is on solid ground in one respect, but not on others. It is obviously very hard for a president or any person to change his basic psychology in response to a singular event, one that took place within the space of a few minutes. In that respect Rove is right. Bush was not a transformed person after that second plane hit the World Trade Center, but I would argue that he was a different one.

Before 9/11, Bush had many domestic policy ambitions, and several major foreign ones. After 9/11, all those competing priorities were reframed through a policy lens of singular focus: ridding the world, but more specifically

the United States, of the scourge of terrorism internationally and domestically. . . .

Before 9/11, Bush's irreverent, sometimes impish
humor was frequently on display. After 9/11, it receded to
the periphery replaced by a deadly seriousness of purpose.
[A journalist] reports that while Bush

> still cannot resist a joke or two (even ribald ones),
> dozens of friends and advisers who have spent time
> with Mr. Bush said in interviews that since Sept. 11 he
> has conducted himself far more seriously than he had
> before. Friends say that while Mr. Bush usually appears
> outwardly upbeat and is trying to convey a sense of nor-
> malcy the terrorist attacks have weighed on the fifty-
> five-year-old president far more than the lowest mo-
> ments of the grueling presidential campaign.

Questions had arisen regarding Bush's level of, and
even capacity for, *gravitas*—that sense of presence, standing, and authority so necessary to leaders wishing to command attention and stimulate compliance. In the hours
following 9/11, a number of commentators, many critics,
saw Bush as barely filling his role. [Howard] Fineman
wrote in *Newsweek:*

> Bush has yet to find a note of eloquence in his own
> voice. He is, in fact, distrustful of it, and went for Texas
> plain talk, rhetoric as flat as the prairie and as blunt as a
> Clint Eastwood soliloquy . . . he did not look larger than
> life at his Oval Office desk, or even particularly com-
> fortable there.

Howard Rosenberg, a reporter for the *Los Angeles
Times*, called Bush stiff and boyish, writing that "Bush has
lacked size in front of the camera when he should have
been commanding and filling the screen with a formidable
presence; even his body language is troubling." Al Hunt,

writing in the *Wall Street Journal*, said that George W. Bush's first address to Congress was "perfectly fine," but "he doesn't fill a room or a chamber." A *Newsweek* editorial noted that other leaders such as Mayor Rudy Giuliani of New York had more presidential presence.

A short time later, Bush appeared before a national audience in a prime time live news conference. In an editorial entitled "Mr. Bush's New Gravitas," the *New York Times* said:

> The George W. Bush who addressed the nation at a prime-time news conference yesterday appeared to be a different man from the one who was just barely elected president last year, or even the man who led the country a month ago. He seemed more confident, determined, and sure of his purpose and was in full command of the complex array of political and military challenges that he faces in the wake of the terrible terrorist attacks of Sept. 11. It was for the most part a reassuring performance that gave comfort to an uneasy nation . . . He's better at it than he and his aides think.

Finding His Voice

Bush had found his voice as he moved from struggling to enact his political vision in a divided contentious society to a leader pursuing the larger purpose of a national mission.

In short, Bush did not become a new man after 9/11, but he certainly became a different one. It is not possible here to explore fully the ways in which Bush's psychology was affected by the events of 9/11. Nonetheless, with no claim to comprehensiveness or exclusivity, it is possible to begin developing a framework for such an analysis—especially as it relates to the foreign policy dimension of his presidency. I briefly examine those elements of interior psychology and leadership skills that seem at this point most relevant to understanding Bush's approach to foreign policy decision making and leadership.

To the student of political psychology, a president's articulated policies, however controversial or traditional, must be reflected in and gauged against his actual behavior. This task actually involves comparing what a president says with what he actually does. We do so not because we expect that he will be a slave to stated policy regardless of circumstances, but rather to gauge, over time and circumstance, whether he acts in ways that are consistent with the views and principles he has espoused. Strongly articulated principles of foreign policy engagement, like their domestic counterparts, raise the issue of whether the president is not only able to have convictions, but also to have the courage of them.

Patriotism

Bush appears to be a real, traditional patriot. He is unabashedly proud of the United States, clearly feels that its virtues easily outweigh its failures, respects its traditions and institutions, and takes seriously and personally his oath to protect and preserve. Bush is not the only president to have many of these feelings, but it is rare to have a president display them so openly and often. Bush's campaign theme stressing the need to bring honor back to the White House obviously had a strategic dimension. It underscored his difference from [former president Bill] Clinton. Yet it was very much more than just that and to miss that fact would be to miss something very important about Bush and his presidency.

Bush's love for this country is palpable, and, as with some other of his emotions, he wears it on his sleeve. Before 9/11, you could read through transcripts of his talks and interviews and repeatedly come upon his expression of how proud he was to serve the country and represent it. It was "a huge honor to represent America overseas." Or, "It's an honor to represent our nation in foreign capitals and be with foreign leaders." One could cite many, many more such sentiments. The point here is that while many presidents might have felt it, Bush says it—often. If the same words, spoken repeatedly in different circumstances, are any indication, he truly believes it.

The First 9/11 Speech

Author and columnist Bill Sammon presents Bush's thoughts as he prepared his first official comments on the September 11, 2001, attacks.

"We're at war," Bush announced.

He jettisoned the education speech he had been scheduled to deliver. Americans needed to hear directly from their president about the tragedy. The press was already waiting for him in the school's library, where two hundred students, parents, school officials, and local dignitaries had been gathered for hours.

[White House Press Secretary Ari] Fleischer and [White House Communication Director Dan] Bartlett hastily drafted a statement, but Bush wanted to change it and put it into his own words. Using his Sharpie, he scribbled three sheets of notes on crinkly white paper. He gathered them up, got to his feet, and headed for the library.

"I remember I had to convince myself to be as calm and resolute as possible, because I knew people were watching," the president told me later.

"I can be an emotional guy. And I was worried, emotional, about loss of life, because the magnitude of what had happened had come home. And at the same time, I knew I needed to send a sense of, you know, calm in the face of what could be panic. And I think I was able to achieve that.

Bill Sammon, *Fighting Back: The War on Terrorism from Inside the Bush White House.* Washington, DC: Regnery, 2002, p. 94.

Given the depth of these feelings and the large role they play in shaping Bush's approach to the presidency, the terrorist attack of 9/11 could not have failed to cause him great personal anguish. But it also had the effect of providing strong emotional fuel to an already high level of resolve, framed by an intense focus on bringing those responsible, and their allies, to justice. After 9/11, Bush said that the war on terrorism was *the* focus of his presidency. These were not just the words of a leader whose country had been attacked. They were the words of a man, also president, forced to experience the vicious, unprovoked, and successful assault of a venerated object of his affections.

I think Bush's deep patriotism specifically expressed as love of country is one explanation for both his measurable rise in gravitas and his sense of mission. Gravitas reflects seriousness of purpose and a corresponding commitment that must be taken seriously by others. Bush is by nature a man with a sense of humor, but there is nothing humorous about these circumstances. The stakes could not be higher, and he recognized them for what they are: matters of life and death for this country.

National Interest

America's interest is the primary prism through which Bush filters foreign policy debates. Yes, it is true that national interest is not always clear. It is also certainly true that one person's view of national interest is another's grave policy mistake. It is also true that "national interest" is complex, and that there are debates about what, exactly, that means in specific circumstances. Yet, on a number of issues, Bush—and his advisers—have very strong views on what these interests are.

Among the many such views that Bush articulated during his campaign were the following:

1. The military was below adequate capability and needed to be strengthened.

2. The military was ill focused and ill configured, too oriented toward past conflicts and not sufficiently oriented to future ones.
3. There was too much emphasis on multilateral commitments, which, as a result, thinned out America's resources and ability to deal with problems of primary national interest.
4. Western values of economic and personal freedom are the foundation of our strength domestically—but also abroad—and trade, democracy, and free market systems are the best vehicles with which to address issues of poverty and economic development.
5. The United States has too many nuclear weapons and can therefore take steps, unilaterally, if necessary, to reduce them.
6. There is too much reliance on treaties that limit the compliant and not the cheaters.
7. In some ways because of the end of the cold war, the world is still a very dangerous place—full of unstable, violent regimes, some of which would like to humble if not destroy us.
8. As a result of issue 7, the United States had to take immediate steps to protect itself with steps ranging from creating an antiballistic missile (ABM) defense system to reviewing American defense postures and developing oil resources to decrease dependency.

Many, if not all of these views, were fiercely debated before the terrorist attack of September 11 and will most likely be debated again. However, it cannot be said that they are vague. Indeed, several points (2, 3, 7, and 8) were, in view of 9/11, prescient. Certainly, they are a clear statement of the administration's view of its definitions of national interest in these times and circumstances.

These strong views of national interest have fueled many of the policy debates and criticisms that have surrounded the Bush presidency. An ABM system? It's needed and the sooner we begin to work on it, the safer America will become. The ABM treaty? It's antiquated, a relic, and a leftover from a time with difficult circumstances. Global warming and the Kyoto Treaty? It isn't possible to support a treaty that will impose huge costs on the American economy—and by extension on those domestically and internationally who depend on its robustness. Nor can a serious treaty to reduce global warming ignore developing countries such as China and India.

Internationalist?

Bush's decision to turn his back on what he and, it should be remembered, the Senate saw as a fatally flawed climate treaty was one of several such instances. His decision not to send a high-level U.S. delegation to the United Nations–sponsored World Conference against Racism, Xenophobia, and Related Prejudice was another. And there were the ABM treaty from which Bush subsequently formally withdrew, the decision to reject a Draft Enforcement Plan for 1972 Ban on Biological Weapons, a decision not to submit an international convention establishing a permanent international tribunal to the U.S. Senate for ratification, the decision to continue the ban on U.S. participation in the Nuclear Test Ban Treaty that the Senate had refused to ratify in 2000, and his public reluctance to commit U.S. military forces to police duties. All of these decisions have been viewed and criticized by many as a by-product of Bush's unilateral style—hence the term "cowboy politics."

Discussions of Bush's "unilateral style" were temporarily suspended after the attack of September 11. Former critics hailed the president's willingness and ability to develop a broad-based coalition to fight terrorists. Bush, it was said, had learned that he could not act independently and that he had recognized out of America's hour of necessity that he needed allies.

Well, yes and no. In an interview with the *Washington Post*, Secretary of Defense Donald Rumsfeld had this to say about the administration's strategy of working with allies:

> Q: I'd like to turn now if we could to some questions about your stewardship of the war. The first is this long-winded question here about turning points in the war. . . .
>
> Rumsfeld: First would be the September 11th attack. . . . *Another key turning point was the decision that we would not have a single coalition but rather we would use floating coalitions or multiple coalitions* and recognize that because this would be long, because it would be difficult, and because different countries have different circumstances, different perspectives and different problems, that we needed their help on a basis that they were comfortable giving it to us and we should not, ought not, and do not expect everyone to do everything. And that's fine. So if someone wants to help in this way but not that, that's fair enough. The critical element of that is that that way the mission determines the coalition. The opposite of that would be if the coalition determined the mission. Once you allow the coalition to determine the mission, whatever you do gets watered down and inhibited so narrowly that you can't really accomplish, you run the risk of not being able to accomplish those things that you really must accomplish. That was an important decision it seems to me. October 7th [2001] really, simply happened to be the day that the bombing started [in Afghanistan].

Unilateralist

Two different, sometimes confounded, strands of criticism are implicit in the view of Bush as a "unilateratist." The first is that Bush goes his own way regardless of what allies suggest. The implication here is that his critics' policy suggestions are superior to his. The accuracy of these criticisms turns on the relative weight of advantages and disadvantages viewed from the perspective of the different national interests involved. Criticism of the fact that Bush followed his own assessment is not in itself evidence of the superiority of either his or his critics' positions.

It is true that Bush and his administration have come to a number of decisions that run counter to widely prevailing views. This has led to the second strand of the unilateralist criticism, which is that Bush is wrong to reject others' advice because they are allies and presumably would be upset in not having their views acted upon. Implicit in this criticism is the view that others' views of what you should do take precedence over your own assessments if they differ, or that you ought to defer in such cases out of a sense of collegiality. The latter psychology is the basis of the well-known syndrome of groupthink or concurrence seeking, which is almost universally viewed as the basis for fundamentally flawed decision making.

International collegiality, or the lack thereof, is not synonymous with good judgment. It *may* reflect good judgment to go along with a high-quality decision that others see that way as well. It may well reflect very poor judgment to go along with a decision about which you have substantial reasonable doubts.

Moreover, the unilateralist label that has been applied to Bush does not fully or fairly describe the range of his international relations. Bush has been a very strong supporter of international trade. Trade by its nature requires collective action, and the rules that govern require widespread agreements and working partnerships. In addition, well before 9/11, he reached out in partnership to countries such as Mexico that have had an ambivalent relationship with the United States and India, with which the United States has had a cool relationship.

Bush is also a man who has placed tremendous stock in his relationships with a number of foreign leaders. He has genuinely embraced Mexico's Vicente Fox as a friend and policy partner. Earlier on, he embraced Russia's President Vladimir Putin as someone with whom he could deal—

and he was right. His relationship with British Prime Minister Tony Blair is extremely close.

If Bush is a unilateralist, he is a very unusual one. His very notable tendency to reach out to varied leaders for policy and political partnerships on foreign policy issues of mutual concern is certainly inconsistent with that view. So is the same pattern that has been noticeable in Bush's relationships in Congress, where he has forged a number of diverse and different bipartisanship partnerships to address particular policy issues (e.g., tax reform, education).

There are two aspects to Bush's approach to his responsibilities as commander in chief that are critical to understanding President Bush, one growing out of how he frames them, and the other a complementary dimension rooted in his psychology. The first is anchored in his belief that America's national interest should be the first and primary, though not necessarily the only, prism through which issues should be considered. That view is clearly reflected in the president's decisions noted earlier regarding various treaties. It is also clearly and strongly reflected in Rumsfeld's remarks about the administration's approach to its allies in the war against terrorism.

The second, more deeply embedded psychological anchor is Bush's approach to relationships. I have suggested elsewhere that a president's or any person's ways of dealing with the myriad relationships they have reflect something very basic and very important about their psychologies. The psychoanalyst Karen Horney had long ago noted that people could move toward, away, or against others, but they can also stand apart from others.

Bush is clearly a man who moves toward others. Yet, he is not a man who needs to be liked and thus tied to others' approval. He can stand to be apart from others. When he said, "I'm a loving guy, and I'm also someone, however, who's got a job to do, and I intend to do it," he captured both elements of his interpersonal psychology quite well.

The Decision to Invade Iraq

Ivo H. Daalder and James M. Lindsay

Bush ordered American forces to attack Iraq on March 19, 2003, asserting that the regime of Saddam Hussein possessed weapons of mass destruction, supported international terrorist groups, and was a brutal and evil dictator. While American forces easily defeated the Iraqi military and were able to capture Hussein, a continuing insurgency by Hussein loyalists, terrorists, and anti-American Muslim groups has undermined U.S. efforts to promote democracy and stability in the country.

Ivo H. Daalder and James M. Lindsay contend in the following selection that the problems faced by America in Iraq after the war were the result of Bush's inability to convince key countries—such as France, Russia, and Germany—to support the invasion. As a result, the United States found itself with only limited international support, mainly from staunch allies such as Great Britain, the authors maintain. Daalder is a senior fellow in foreign policy studies at the Brookings Institute and the author of a number of books on international security. Lindsay is vice president and director of the Council on Foreign Relations. Both previously served as staff members on the National Security Council.

A LTHOUGH IRAQ WAS DESTINED TO BE A TARGET OF ACtion, debate over how to cope with the growing vio-

Ivo H. Daalder and James M. Lindsay, *America Unbound: The Bush Revolution in Foreign Policy*. Washington, DC: Brookings Institute, 2003. Copyright © 2003 by The Brookings Institution. All rights reserved. Reproduced by permission.

lence between Israel and the Palestinians absorbed the administration's energies during the first half of 2002. . . .

The months of debate about the Middle East had left the administration's Iraq policy adrift. There had been no follow-up to Bush's decision [following the September 11, 2001, terrorist attacks] that Saddam had to be taken out. Even many of the administration's senior officials were in the dark. When Richard Haass, [Secretary of State Colin] Powell's close confidant, met with [National Security Adviser Condoleza] Rice in July in one of their regular meetings, he wondered whether Iraq really should be front and center in the administration's foreign policy. "That decision's been made, don't waste your breath," Haass recalled Rice's saying. Yet, aside from military planning, which had in one form or another been going on since mid-September 2001, the policy process on Iraq was at a standstill.

Focus on Iraq

That process finally got under way in July. During a series of secretive meetings among Bush's top advisers, which appeared as "Regional Strategies Meeting" on the private schedules of the participants so as to hide their true nature, the administration began to tackle a host of critical questions. What role, if any, should there be for the United Nations, which for the past twelve years had dominated Iraq policy? Should resumption of weapons inspections be a goal? What could key allies contribute? What were the military options for removing Saddam? What would come after his ouster? Should Congress be asked to authorize the use of force? The idea was to use the summer months to hash out these and other questions and to begin a rollout of Bush's policy after Labor Day. Nothing much could be done publicly because, as [Bush's adviser] Karl Rove noted, "in August the president is sort of on vacation." Moreover, said [Chief of Staff] Andrew Card, "from a marketing point of view, you don't introduce new products in August."

However, maintaining an orderly, politically sensitive process is not the same as agreeing how to launch a new product—especially when the "product" is a major war thousands of miles from home. There were deep differences within the administration on how to proceed, with Powell and Cheney representing the competing poles in the debate. Powell, who had done yeoman's work pulling together a large and broad antiterror coalition, wanted "something approaching that level of support if we were going to do Iraq." During a two-hour private dinner with Bush in early August, Powell argued that Bush should go to the United Nations and seek international backing for a vigorous weapons inspection regime. The president should consider using force only if Baghdad refused to turn over its weapons of mass destruction, as demanded by sixteen successive Security Council resolutions. Cheney, in contrast, feared that the UN route would once again open up the inspection trap, in which Saddam would give the weapons inspectors just enough to undermine efforts to gain international support for military action. In any case, the vice president argued, international support was not critical. "The fact of the matter is for most of the others who are engaged in this debate, they don't have the capability to do anything about it anyway." Moreover, Cheney had no doubt that in the long run, after Saddam had been successfully ousted, "a good part of the world, especially our allies, will come around to our way of thinking."

Opposition

This internal debate burst into public view during what Powell recalled was far more "exciting an August" than he had anticipated. On Capitol Hill, the Senate Foreign Relations Committee held a series of hearings that proved unexpectedly critical of a possible war against Iraq—with leading Republican members among those who questioned the wisdom of acting precipitously. Also chiming in was

House Republican Majority Leader Dick Armey, who argued that it was unbecoming of America's great tradition to attack another country without provocation. "I don't believe that America will justifiably make an unprovoked attack on another nation," Armey told reporters in early August. "It would not be consistent with what we have been as a nation or what we should be as a nation." Asked what America should do about the threat Saddam posed, he said: "My own view would be to let him bluster, let him rant and rave all he wants and let that be a matter between he and his own country. As long as he behaves himself within his own borders, we should not be addressing any attack or resources against him."

But the most unexpected criticism came from a number of high-ranking officials in previous Republican administrations, some no doubt encouraged by protagonists inside the administration, all of whom argued strongly for seeking a broad international coalition to support action against Iraq. James Baker, the elder Bush's close friend and his first secretary of state, argued that the president should go to the United Nations and seek another resolution in support of squeezing Saddam. Henry Kissinger, while supporting the need for action against Iraq, maintained that in order to gain international support, "the objective of regime change should be subordinated in American declaratory policy to the need to eliminate weapons of mass destruction from Iraq as required by the U.N. resolutions." Brent Scowcroft, the senior Bush's former national security adviser and the coauthor of his memoirs, went further. He argued that "an attack on Iraq at this time would seriously jeopardize, if not destroy, the global counterterrorist campaign we have undertaken." Lawrence Eagleburger, who had replaced Baker as secretary of state, took the same position.

The escalating opposition to war against Iraq from prominent Republicans left the administration's pro-war camp reeling. But not for long. In a major speech in late August before the Veterans of Foreign Wars, Cheney made the most detailed and powerful case yet for taking action against Iraq. He warned that the problem was not just that Saddam Hussein possessed chemical and biological weapons and was ready to use them. The threat was more dire still. "Many of us are convinced that Saddam will acquire nuclear weapons fairly soon," Cheney warned. "Just how soon, we cannot really gauge. Intelligence is an uncertain business, even in the best of circumstances." But the consequences of Saddam's succeeding would be grave. . . .

Cheney's speech elicited just the reaction he had intended. It caused an uproar all over Europe—accelerating German chancellor Gerhard Schröder's decision to make opposition to America's Iraq policy the centerpiece of his reelection campaign and leading French president Jacques Chirac to condemn "attempts to legitimize the unilateral and preemptive use of force." More important, Cheney's speech blind-sided Powell, who was then on vacation in the Hamptons. Bob Woodward recorded Powell's reaction when he read the front-page headline "Cheney Says Peril of Nuclear Iraq Justifies Attack" in the next day's New York Times. "Powell was astonished. It seemed like a preemptive attack" on the policy process. Ten days earlier, Powell, Cheney, and the president's other top advisers had met with Bush and unanimously agreed to take the Iraq issue to the United Nations. Cheney's swipe at inspections was also contrary to Bush's year-long insistence that inspectors should return to Iraq, a point Powell himself had made publicly in a prerecorded BBC interview days earlier. "The president has been clear that he believes weapons inspectors should return," he had told David Frost. "Iraq has been in violation of many UN resolutions for most of the last 11 or so years. And so, as a first step, let's see what the inspectors find."

With the internal debate now public, Bush was forced to choose. This he did in early September, when he essentially decided to take Powell's route to Cheney's goal. The president would go to the United Nations and challenge the members to enforce the numerous Security Council resolutions passed on Iraq over the preceding twelve years. "All the world now faces a test, and the United Nations a difficult and defining moment," Bush told the General Assembly in mid-September. "Are Security Council resolutions to be honored and enforced, or cast aside without consequence? Will the United Nations serve the purpose of its founding, or will it be irrelevant?" If meeting that challenge required the Security Council to enact new resolutions, so be it. "But the purposes of the United States should not be doubted," the president warned. "The Security Council resolutions will be enforced—the just demands of peace and security will be met—or action will be unavoidable. And a regime that has lost its legitimacy will also lose its power." It was a bold speech that challenged the world community. It was nevertheless received with great relief by many countries. The United States had decided to work through the United Nations rather than to act alone.

Despite Bush's portentous speech, the administration had no strategy for turning its challenge to the world into a workable policy. The decision to seek a new UN resolution had been made only hours before Bush ascended to the podium in the General Assembly. For days, Cheney had vigorously resisted going to the United Nations yet again on Iraq, but Bush finally decided to side with Powell on this issue, not least because Prime Minister Tony Blair had told him that Britain could support the United States in war only if the issue were enforcement of UN resolutions. Yet no one knew what such a resolution should contain. An interagency team charged with drafting a text started work only after Bush had spoken in New York. When Iraq predictably reacted to Bush's speech by announcing that UN inspectors could return "unconditionally," Washington was still trying to get its act together.

The internal policy battle that had preceded Bush's UN

address now shifted to the drafting of a new resolution. There was broad agreement that any resolution would have to declare Iraq in material breach of existing UN demands to disarm, contain a tough new inspection regime that would give weapons inspectors full and unfettered access to all sites at any time, and warn that force might be used if Baghdad failed to comply. But Pentagon officials, backed by Cheney's office, wanted more. They insisted that the resolution authorize weapons inspectors to declare no-fly/no-drive zones and other exclusion zones that would be "enforced by UN security forces or member states," in effect granting the United States a right to intervene militarily in support of the inspection process. They also insisted that in case of Iraqi noncompliance, the resolution authorize "member states to use all necessary means to restore international peace and security in the area."

A draft resolution containing the Pentagon's provisions was circulated in New York in late September, even though the State Department and Britain had argued that it stood no chance of being accepted by the other permanent members of the Security Council. Indeed, the draft went nowhere. France, Russia, and China were willing to consider tougher inspections (itself a major change), but rejected any preauthorization for the use of force, whether to assist the inspectors or to punish noncompliance. There could be, in the parlance of the UN negotiators, "no automaticity" with regard to any use of force.

Behind this firm stance lay the growing conviction on the part of many Security Council members that the United States had come to the United Nations under false pretenses. Many believed that Washington regarded the resolution as a prelude to war rather than as a possible alternative to it. The Bush administration provided plenty of ammunition for this view. Even as it was circulating a draft resolution demanding Iraq give up all its weapons of mass destruction, Powell told the BBC that "the U.S. continues to believe that the best way to disarm Iraq is through a regime change." Subsequent clarifications by Bush and Powell—that, as Bush argued, Saddam's full compliance with UN resolutions "would also change the nature of the Iraqi regime itself"—did little to alleviate doubts about the administration's true intentions.

UN Politics

With America as much as Iraq becoming the issue at the United Nations, there was no way a majority in the Security Council would support a resolution authorizing the use of force if the United States or anyone else aside from the Security Council itself determined Baghdad had failed to comply. To prove the point, France threatened to introduce its own draft resolution that would strengthen inspections but remain silent on consequences in case of noncompliance. Faced with a likely Security Council majority in favor of such a resolution, Washington was forced to compromise. Rather than approving an automatic authorization to use force in case Iraq failed to comply, the new resolution agreed that the Security Council would convene to "consider the situation." Separately, Baghdad was warned of "serious consequences" if it continued to violate its obligations under various UN resolutions. That formulation proved crucial. Paris, Moscow, and others had successfully resisted any automaticity. But Washington and London had successfully avoided the need to go back to the Security Council for an affirmative vote to use force.

After eight weeks of intense negotiations, the UN Security Council voted unanimously to adopt resolution 1441 on November 8, 2002. It was a remarkable victory for America—and for Powell. Three years earlier, when the Security Council last considered how to deal with Iraq's weapons of mass destruction, France, Russia, and China had abstained on a U.S.–UK resolution that in many ways proposed weakening the inspection regime from what had existed before.

Now, a much stronger regime than had ever been in place received the Council's unanimous approval. As for Powell, he had won important internal battles—on whether to go to the United Nations, to seek a new resolution, and to compromise on the authorization to use force. And he had worked hard to persuade his colleagues on the Security Council to back a much more robust approach to getting Iraq into compliance with its international obligations.

Nevertheless, even as the administration savored its victory in New York, it again failed to anticipate the many pitfalls that were sure to arise once the provisions of resolution 1441 were implemented. To win agreement, Washington had had to settle for a resolution that postponed rather than resolved many of the most critical issues. For example, there was no consensus within the Security Council on how much Iraqi cooperation would be enough to avoid war—nor on how much noncooperation would provoke it. Nor was there a prescribed timeline or a clear sense of how long inspectors should probe to determine Iraqi compliance. Bush's advisers were divided on these issues. Many assumed that robust inspections fed by U.S. and British intelligence would quickly provide a "smoking gun" proving that Saddam was cheating or that he would blatantly refuse to cooperate with the inspectors. At that point everyone, including France, would support the use of force to topple the regime. Short of finding such convincing evidence, however, the administration was not prepared to deal with situations in which differing interpretations about Iraq's compliance would come to the fore.

Iraq Responds

A month after the resolution's passage, Baghdad delivered a 12,000-page declaration on its banned weapons program. The declaration was anything but the "currently accurate, full, and complete" listing of its programs that resolution 1441 required. Baghdad's failure to come clean signaled to everyone in the administration—including Powell—that Saddam had no intention of taking advantage of his final opportunity to disarm. "It should be obvious that the pattern of systematic holes and gaps in Iraq's declaration is not the result of accidents or editing oversights or technical mistakes," Powell declared. "These are material omissions that, in our view, constitute another material breach." War now appeared inevitable—indeed, sooner rather than later.

But few other countries shared Washington's conclusion about the inevitability of war—though many had long believed that this had been its objective all along. French diplomats argued that a further material breach was defined by the resolution as occurring when there are "false statements or omissions in the declarations . . . and [not or] failure by Iraq at any time to comply with and fully cooperate in the implementation" of the resolution. In other words, a false declaration alone was not enough to justify force. But that, clearly, was not Washington's view, and this became abundantly clear to Paris when Chirac's diplomatic adviser, Maurice Gourdault-Montagne, met with Rice in Washington in mid-January. Back in Paris, he told Chirac that Bush was going to war "no matter what." It was a course France could not, at least not yet, support.

Stumbling Toward War

For Washington, then, the question was not whether to go to war, but how to ensure the broadest possible international support. And it is here that diplomacy failed most spectacularly. Blair had served notice that Britain's support hinged on further Security Council action, preferably a second resolution, a position shared by many other European countries. An opening was provided in late January [2003], when Hans Blix, one of the chief UN weapons inspectors, bluntly criticized Baghdad's halting cooperation in his first report to the Security Council since inspections had resumed two months earlier. "Iraq appears not to have come to a genuine acceptance, not even today, of the disarmament which was demanded of it." Four days after Blix's surprise statement, Blair met Bush at the White House and pressed for the introduction of a second resolution. Bush declined.

This proved to be a mistake. For in response, perhaps, to Blix's critical report, Baghdad shifted its behavior. Cooperation on inspections and other procedural matters improved, and Iraq even began to destroy more than one hundred Al-Samoud missiles that Blix declared to be in violation of the range limitations for ballistic missiles permitted by the United Nations. Blix's subsequent reports to the Security Council were far more measured in tone than his initial, unexpectedly harsh indictment of Baghdad. Blix instead stressed Iraqi cooperation on procedures and process, even if on substance many questions remained unresolved. Also, just as Cheney and others opposed to resuming inspections had predicted, the political momentum in New York shifted away from Washington toward the bloc of member states, led by France and Germany, that opposed war.

It was only on February 24 that the United States, Britain, and Spain introduced a second resolution declaring that Iraq had failed to meet its obligations. Last-minute negotiations seeking to add specific benchmarks and a timeline followed, but to no avail. Washington had little interest in being flexible—the only reason it backed another resolution was to help Britain and other friends who needed it for domestic political reasons. It expended little effort to secure the resolution's passage. Powell worked the phones, but he did not travel to any of the critical countries to secure their vote. Nothing was done to try to woo Russia or even Germany away from France, which by early March had indicated it would veto a resolution authorizing war "regardless of the circumstances," as Chirac put it. Washington even failed to put significant pressure on Mexico or Chile—two other Security Council members—to side with the United States.

On March 6 Bush made one last bravura stance. "No matter what the whip count is, we're calling for the vote," Bush told a primetime news conference. "It's time for people to show their cards, to let the world know where they stand when it comes to Saddam." But it was too late. A second resolution would not only fail because of a French and likely Russian veto; there were not even the votes necessary for Washington and London to claim a moral victory. The admission of failure came at a strange summit between the leaders of Britain, Spain, and the United States in the Azores, a group of small islands in the Atlantic, on March 16. Nothing could have underscored these leaders' international isolation more graphically than this meeting in the middle of nowhere. "It was seen as a defeat," Powell later conceded, "and it was a defeat."

Thus when the United States went to war against Iraq on March 19, it did so without the explicit backing of the UN Security Council. Perhaps there was nothing the Bush administration could have done to avoid this outcome. It would have been difficult to overcome the widespread presumption at the United Nations and elsewhere that Washington was bent on regime change in Baghdad, no matter what. Then again, a more vigorous diplomacy and greater tactical acumen might have succeeded in gaining the consensus of the Council—or at least of a large majority of its members. For example, had Bush agreed with Blair in late January and introduced a second resolution setting out the remaining disarmament tasks necessary for Iraq to fulfill by a clear deadline (for instance, eight weeks hence), he might have won passage of a resolution before opposition to it hardened. But even if it had proved impossible to pass such a resolution, the effort would likely have had the political benefit of isolating those who were unalterably opposed, instead of isolating Washington.

Bush's Policies Have Made America Less Secure Against Terrorism

Edward S. Herman

In the following selection, Edward S. Herman argues that George W. Bush's national security policies have undermined the safety of Americans. Bush's failure to take the threat of terrorism seriously early in his presidency resulted in the catastrophic attacks of September 11, 2001, according to Herman. Since then, in Herman's opinion, Bush and his team have done little to protect the nation against further attack while stoking fear among the public in order to shore up political support. Furthermore, the American-led wars in Afghanistan and Iraq have provoked massive anti-American sentiments worldwide and in turn have produced a new cohort of terrorists who oppose the United States.

Herman is an economist, author, and media analyst and is professor emeritus of finance at the Wharton School of the University of Pennsylvania.

O NE OF THE REMARKABLE PHENOMENA IN THIS CRAZY PO-
litical environment has been the Republican administration's success in getting President George [W.]

Edward S. Herman, "George Bush Versus U.S. National Security," *Z Magazine*, October 2003. Copyright © 2003 by *Z Magazine*. Reproduced by permission.

Bush portrayed as the person who the citizenry can rely on to protect their security interests. This is amazing, given the Bush record and plans. I will argue that he has been a calamitous failure on security issues up to now [October 2003] and that he is busily engaged in sowing the seeds for security disasters in the future. In saying this I am using security in the narrow sense, concerned only with threats of terrorist and military attack. If we extend the concept to encompass the security of the U.S. citizenry from threats of unemployment, pension loss, lack of medical insurance, street crime, security state abuses of civil liberties, breakdowns in electrical, water, or transportation service, or damage to health resulting from environmental degradation, the Bush threat to security is overwhelming.

Bush has gotten away with this image of security-savior by stoking fears, stirring up patriotic ardor, manufacturing wars—or rather invasions of small and virtually defenseless countries—and strutting about looking very grave, pronouncing momentous words attempting to evoke Churchillian grandeur ("I will not yield; I will not rest; I will not relent in waging this struggle for freedom and security for the American people"), and acting his part in frequent photo-ops that portray the erstwhile draft-dodger as an active warrior chieftain (his jet-landing in Air Force garb on the USS *Abraham Lincoln* [May 1, 2003]).

But he couldn't have done this without an ultra-compliant media that followed his agenda, featured virtually without comment his photo-ops, serial misrepresentations of fact, promoted scares, and refused to challenge their leader, serving him much in the manner of the media of a totalitarian state. Professor Lance Bennett refers to this media performance as a "near-perfect journalistic participation in government propaganda operations." The large right-wing segment of the media have functioned as literal press agents and cheerleaders for the Bush administration, setting the tone and helping cow the "liberal" sector of the corporate media into similar, if less vocal, subservience to the government (although most of them didn't need to be cowed). At a deeper level, this reflects the fact that the corporate community is very pleased with the Bush administration, which has been brazenly aggressive in providing business tax breaks, resource giveaways, reductions in environmental controls, cutbacks in the welfare state, and impediments to labor organization. Such service to the needs of the powerful feeds into the performance of the corporate and advertiser-funded media, which treats a Bush much differently than a [Bill] Clinton, [Al] Gore, or any other politician who may try hard to placate business, but is not prepared for 100 percent corporate service.

The 9/11 Security Failure

The Bush administration was directly responsible for the [security failure that led to the September 11, 2001, attacks], one of the greatest and most inexcusable in U.S. history. The Administration had been warned by the outgoing Clinton team of the [terrorist group] al Qaeda threat and essentially ignored that warning in its eight months in office before 9/11. The Administration failed to take any action based on a host of subsequent warning signals, including information on the flight training of suspicious individuals and explicit advisories of a threatened "spectacular" terrorist action provided by the intelligence agencies of half-a dozen allied countries. Bush's August 6, 2001 intelligence briefing included an item, "Bin Laden Determined to Strike in US," which noted the "FBI judgment about pattern of activity consistent with preparation for hijackings and other types of attack." The Bush administration did nothing in response to these warnings in the way of checking out threatening "patterns of activity" like flight training or trying to strengthen airport security. On September 10, 2001, Attorney-General John Ashcroft submitted a Justice Department budget that reduced by $58 million FBI requests that would have provided for 149 counterterrorism field agents, 200 intelligence analysts, and 54 translators; and he proposed a $65 million cut for state and local governments for counterterrorism supplies, including radios and decontamination equipment. Ashcroft's priorities did not include terrorism; they featured "securing the rights of victims of crimes," immigration control, dealing with drug trafficking, and the threat of prostitutes in Louisiana.

The failure to deal with the al Qaeda terror threat may well have been connected to the relationships between the Bush family, friends, and oil interests and the Saudis, including members of the bin Laden family, some of whom were allowed to leave the country in the immediate wake of 9/11 with White House approval—while large numbers of Arabs with no known connections to bin Laden or al Qaeda were quickly rounded up for questioning, frequent mistreatment, and open-ended incarceration. The Bush administration went to great pains to impede and delay an investigation of the 9/11 security failure, refusing access to [national security adviser] Condoleezza Rice, many CIA and other personnel, as well as executive documents and, in the end, insisting on keeping from public scrutiny the 28 pages of the long-delayed report on the reasons for the security failure that dealt with the Saudi connection.

It is an amazing testimony to the power of the right wing that the Bush administration was able to get away with delaying and then successfully censoring the joint congressional committee's 9/11 report and without ever suffering any serious condemnation. Clearly 9/11 has been considered an event of overwhelming importance, with almost 3,000 U.S. dead, generating vast publicity and expressions of grief and anger, and providing the basis for an open-ended "war on terror." Recall also that some of the 19 plane hijackers had even trained in aircraft management in the United States, had coordinated this operation on U.S.

soil without any interference from a security apparatus costing the taxpayers an estimated $30 billion a year. Then there is the record of warnings and evidence of Bush administration disinterest, possibly influenced by the Saudi-oil connection. Then there is the failure of the U.S. alert system to respond to the hijacking, and the evidence that leader George Bush became conspicuous by his absence following his hearing of the Twin Tower hits.

Bush Evades Blame

Many of the 9/11 victims' families have been appalled at the security failure cover-up and some have even pursued the issue with a great deal of energy. But the media have been exceedingly quiet and from 9/11 to the present they have exerted little pressure on the Administration to explain their failure and they have not suggested. that this dereliction of duty constitutes criminal and impeachable negligence. At the height of the disclosures of Bush's intelligence failures, in May 2002, the *New York Times* editorial stress was on the inability to assemble data and to act as a "chronic" problem and the need to focus on "what really matters, which is preventing another assault" by bin Laden, rather than blame assessment. In fact, the media have hardly admitted 9/11 to be a Bush failure at all—the *Philadelphia Inquirer* made 9/11 something that might taint Clinton's legacy, without even mentioning any possible Bush responsibility.

I would submit that if Clinton had been in office and displayed the same record of non- and mal-performance the media would have been unrelenting, their investigative efforts would have been frenzied, and the security failure would have been pinned on Clinton along with his immediate subordinates. (Dick Cheney, for example, was presented as Bush's "point man on domestic terrorism" in May 2001, but he hadn't lifted a finger in dealing with this responsibility by 9/11.) If Clinton was impeached for lies associated with the Lewinsky scandal,[1] can there be any doubt that he would have been impeached—and convicted and removed from office—for this much more serious crime? But he was not protected by the right wing and "liberal media," as is George Bush, the more aggressive servant of the corporate community.

Security Failure to Fearmongering

Having egregiously failed to protect U.S. national security on 9/11, the Bush team then rushed to the opposite extreme of inflating and manufacturing terrorist threats, stoking fear, and presenting themselves as the security-protectors that the U.S. citizenry could rely upon. This took the heat off their catastrophic failure—and the ongoing corporate and Bush administration's conflict-of-interest scandals—and allowed them to use this new focus and diversion to carry out external and internal policies that they had wanted to pursue but found difficult to implement without a cover.

This new effort to work the security-protector gambit began with an immediate rush of naval vessels to New York harbor and elsewhere, and continuous Air Force flights over New York and other major cities that continued for many months. This was extremely silly, as it should have been obvious even to the editors of the *New York Times* that bin Laden, and even Saddam Hussein, had no navy or air force that might attack New York City, that 9/11 was a long-planned once-off project, and that further terrorist attacks, if they took place, were going to be by low-tech methods. But the media didn't laugh or criticize. They didn't point out the contrast between the failure to deal with the real threat and the idiotic (and wasteful) new rush to convey the image of alert security-protectors. No, they fell

---

1. lying to Congress about his affair with White House intern Monica Lewinsky

in line with that high gullibility quotient they so frequently display when dealing with alleged "security" or foreign policy issues (as they have done in dealing with the Bush pre-invasion claims of Saddam Hussein's threatening weapons of mass destruction).

Thereafter the Bush team made frequent announcements of terror threats and arrests of terror suspects, based on information far less compelling than that which they had completely ignored before 9/11 and often laughable. Ashcroft's claim that the FBI had disrupted a plan to launch a "dirty bomb" [radioactive bomb] attack on Washington by its May 8, 2002 arrest of a former member of a Chicago street gang, soon collapsed when it was revealed that there was no bomb, no access to nuclear material, not even a plan—only an alleged "intention." But the media played this up heavily and they regularly feature general claims of ominous threats, even when timed to coincide with embarrassing political moments for the Bush terror fighters. The new Homeland Security Administration concocted a system of color alerts for terror threats of different levels of seriousness and they were on frequently, dependably at politically convenient moments. These alerts were invariably false alarms. Despite all the fear propaganda, and barring the attacks via the anthrax mailings,[2] there was not a single real terrorist act on U.S. soil for the two years following 9/11. Theoretically this could have been the result of the arrests, alerts and heightened surveillance that had been put in place. The other possibility, which I believe to be the main reality is that al Qaeda was poorly represented in the United States and had temporarily exhausted its capabilities here.

The Bush administration took advantage of the new

---

2. In late 2001 several letters were mailed containing anthrax powder, causing nineteen infections and five fatalities.

fear environment and stoked patriotism to push its National Missile Defense (NMD) and other military projects that had absolutely nothing to do with combating al Qaeda and terrorism, but which neither the media nor Democrats contested. A very large fraction of the new money allocated to "security" after 9/11 went to these non-terrorism-related projects and military attacks abroad that served the semi-hidden Bush agenda of projecting U.S. imperial power on a global basis, and which are reliable producers of more anti-U.S. terrorism.

But while big money was being spent by Bush on NMD and other provocative and wasteful weapons systems, and wars, the Bush team was shortchanging programs that would actually help fend off and protect the public against terrorist acts. It wasted money and effort in putting up a huge Homeland Security bureaucracy, when even a relatively small bureaucracy like that of the FBI had not been able to coordinate information within its own ranks. It has put a great deal of money into increased surveillance, but short-changed the security needs of airports, ports, and other vulnerable infrastructure such as electric and nuclear facilities, and water pumping stations.

Although the front lines of defense against terrorist attacks are the local police, firefighters, and emergency workers, and although many new homeland security duties were placed upon them. U.S. cities have received "only a relative pittance" to fund these activities, and because of Congress's combining new homeland security funds with existing federal monies for crime prevention, public safety, and emergency preparedness. "America's cities and towns actually experienced a net loss in federal support."

The Department of Homeland Security alerts call for action by local emergency providers, although ordinary citizens are free to ignore them. These alerts therefore regularly require overtime payments for local police and others, and the U.S. Conference of Mayors estimates that cities have been spending an additional $70 million per week on personnel costs alone to keep up with Orange Alert demands. [Politician] David Morris points out that "Bush's strategy of distinguishing between local and national security has led to a truly bizarre situation. Whenever the likelihood of a terrorist attack goes up, the capacity of our communities to cope goes down." Add to this the fiscal crisis now besetting states and local governments, with virtually no aid from the Bush administration—which is busy pumping federal resources into military and occupation expenditures and tax cuts for Bush cronies and business supporters—and the local capacity to respond to terrorism is weakened further.

Manufacturing Terrorists

During the Vietnam War the U.S. military displayed its mastery of the art of creating enemies by its racist contempt for the little "yellow dwarves" (Lyndon Johnson) and the lavish use of firepower on "suspected Vietcong villages." This country also used chemicals on a large scale to destroy peasant rice crops (Operation Ranch Hand) The U.S. military succeeded in producing two enemy soldiers for every one they killed, but never quite grasped where these new replacement soldiers were coming from. But not everybody in the military was confused—as U.S. Army Master Sergeant Donald Duncan testified in 1966: "One day I asked one of our Vietnamese helicopter pilots what he thought of the last bomb raid. [He answered] 'I think maybe today we make many Vietcong.'"

George Bush and his cabal have build on this tradition. The United States is using chemical and biological agents against drug-related crops, with spillover to other crops, in Colombia. This is a superb hate- and terrorist-producing operation.

The Bush administration has entered into a close alliance with "man of peace" [Israeli prime minister] Ariel

Sharon and has given virtually unconditional support to Israel's ethnic cleansing, and it is completely unconcerned with Israel's nuclear (and chemical-biological) arsenal and threats while aggressively threatening any Israeli neighbor daring to pursue similar arms. Bush declared an open-ended "war on terror," first announced as a "crusade," with a very obvious anti-Islam bias, but is open to support of any government willing to align with the Bush team in its global projection of power. Many authoritarian governments have been happy to join the war as it has provided them with aid and protection in their own campaigns to attack and crush dissident movements.

The serial wars, first, Afghanistan, then Iraq, with others openly threatened, have been extremely well designed to produce terrorists. In both cases (as in Vietnam), by the lavish use of firepower that killed and injured large numbers of civilians, and by the ground behavior of U.S. troops (beating, handcuffing and blindfolding men, women and children, and shooting to kill at the slightest provocation)—taking numerous prisoners in blind sweeps, treating them badly, and holding them for long periods without charge or ability to communicate with their families. In Afghanistan, large numbers of Taliban prisoners were murdered in prison and in transit to other locations, mainly by U.S. allies but with obvious U.S. acquiescence. There are thousands of prisoners in Iraq whose status and treatment are unclear but whose treatment is in clear violation of international law.

Bush justified the attack on Iraq on the basis of Iraq's alleged providing "training and safe haven to terrorists . . . who would willingly use weapons of mass destruction against America and other peace-loving countries." But as [journalist] Jonathan Freedland has pointed out "With astonishing speed, the United States and Britain are making their nightmares come true. Iraq is fast becoming the land that they warned about. . . ." So while the Bush claim was a lie, "events have taken care of that little lacuna in the US argument."

But it would be a mistake to think that the Bush cabal regrets this wee mistake. They wanted an excuse to invade and occupy and used many lies as justification. Furthermore, I don't believe they are all that upset over the fact that their policies have produced more terrorism, although the difficulty and costs of pacifying Iraq is definitely a setback. But just as 9/11 was a Bush windfall, so further terrorist acts will give him and the cabal the further fear and "security" cover for the continued projection of power abroad and service to the corporate community and military-industrial complex at home. This works because the mainstream media get on each terrorist gambit bandwagon and refuse to point out the self-fulfilling character of the Bush policies in which wholesale terror elicits retail terror. The hope is that the costs of these cruel and dangerous policies, feeding back on ordinary citizens and making them steadily poorer and more insecure, will produce a public enlightenment and outcry that will affect the media and have political consequences.

PRESIDENTS
and their
DECISIONS

CHAPTER

2

HOMELAND
SECURITY

Bush's Homeland Security Policies Threaten Civil Liberties

Nick Gillespie

After the September 11, 2001, terrorist attacks, Bush signed into law the USA PATRIOT Act, which enhances law enforcement powers in an effort to prevent future terrorist attacks. The act grants the FBI greater surveillance powers, such as increased latitude in using wiretaps. According to Nick Gillespie in the following selection, trading freedom and privacy for enhanced security is ill advised. He contends that Americans are sacrificing the values for which America stands by permitting infringements on their basic freedoms. Gillespie argues that when people sacrifice freedom for security in times of crisis, they unwittingly pave the way for ever more restrictions on their civil liberties. Nick Gillespie is *Reason*'s editor in chief.

A MID THE MAD, HORRIFIC CARNAGE OF [THE SEPTEMBER 11, 2001, terrorist attacks on America]—amid the planes screaming into office buildings and cornfields; amid the last-minute phone calls by doomed innocents to loved ones; amid the victims so desperate that they dove from the heights of the World Trade Center to the pavement below (what nightmare thoughts must have shot through their minds in that all too brief yet interminable

Nick Gillespie, "Freedom for Safety: An Old Trade—and a Useless One," *Reason*, October 2002, pp. 25–26. Copyright © 2002 by the Reason Foundation, 3415 S. Sepulveda Blvd., Suite 400, Los Angeles, CA 90034, www.reason.com. Reproduced by permission.

fall to Ground Zero?); amid the billowing cloud of ash that smothered Manhattan and the rest of the country like a volcanic eruption of unmitigated human suffering; amid the heroism of plane passengers and firemen and cops and neighbors; amid the crush of steel and concrete and glass that flattened 220 stories into a pile barely 50 feet tall— amid the 3,000 deaths that day, something else died too.

Trading Freedom for Security

By nightfall, it seemed, we had changed from a nation that placed a uniquely high value on privacy and freedom to one that embraced security and safety as first principles. Of *course* we swapped freedom for safety. Just look again at those people jumping from the twin towers to understand why 78 percent of respondents in a recent Gallup/University of Oklahoma poll favored trading civil liberties for "security" (and why 71 percent supported a national ID card too). Never mind that the trade hasn't made us safer, or that it erodes the freedom that we say is precisely what the terrorists hate about us.

Within days of the attacks, Attorney General John Ashcroft pushed Congress to pass expansive anti-terrorism legislation that was a lawman's wish list (and not very different from the regular requests made by lawmen before 9/11). We *must*, implored the man who had redirected FBI efforts away from counterterrorism and back toward battling drugs and kiddie porn, make it easier for cops and feds and spies to get the drop on suspects, broaden the definition of and increase the penalties for money laundering, impose new restrictions on immigration, and on and on.

On October 26, 2001, President George W. Bush signed the USA PATRIOT Act, an acronym for a law so ludicrously named that it sounds like [satirist] Thomas Pynchon parodying [dystopia author] George Orwell: the Uniting and Strengthening America by Providing Appropriate Tools Required to Intercept and Obstruct Terrorism Act. As the

Electronic Frontier Foundation (EFF) and other critics noted, the legislation ran to 342 pages and made major changes to over a dozen statutes that had limited government surveillance of citizens. We can assume that many legislators and their staffers, in the time-honored tradition, didn't read the text before casting their votes. Likewise, it will be years, not just months, before the act's full implications are clear.

The USA PATRIOT Act is a synecdoche for the freedom-for-safety swap. Among many other things, it sanctioned roving wiretaps (which allow police to track individuals over different phones and computers) and spying on the Web browsers of people who are not even criminal suspects. It rewrote the definitions of terrorism and money laundering to include all sorts of lesser and wider-ranging offenses. More important, as EFF underscored, "In asking for these broad new powers, the government made no showing that the previous powers of law enforcement and intelligence agencies to spy on U.S. citizens were insufficient to allow them to investigate and prosecute acts of terrorism." Nothing that's emerged in the past year contradicts that early assessment.

A Slipperly Slope

"We're likely to experience more restrictions on personal freedom than has ever been the case in this country," pronounced Supreme Court Justice Sandra Day O'Connor last year after visiting Ground Zero. So we have, in ways large and small, profound and trivial. The worst part of the freedom-for-safety swap is that it's *never* a done deal; the safety providers are endless hagglers, always coming back for more. This fall's [2002] major homeland security legislation, unfinished at press time, will doubtless renew the negotiations.

Who knows where it will end? Freedom and privacy rarely, if ever, disappear in one fell swoop. In just a year, we've become accustomed to unnamed "detainees" being held in secret by the Department of Justice (and to the DOJ refusing to comply with state and federal court rulings to release the names of suspects); to the possibility of equally secret "military tribunals" (it's all right—they won't be used against U.S. citizens, except *maybe* "bad apples" like dirty bomb suspect Jose Padilla, and wasn't he a gang member anyway?); to state and federal agencies' dragging their feet on releasing documents legally available through open government laws; and to legislators such as Senator Mike DeWine (R-Ohio) constantly pushing the limits of the USA PATRIOT Act. (DeWine wants to allow the FBI to wiretap legal immigrants on the weakest "suspicion" of criminal activity.)

We Are Not Safer

We've become trained to show up hours earlier to airports and to shuffle passively through security checkpoints, to unbuckle our pants and untuck our shirts, to hold our feet up in the air while agents wave wands over our shoes, to surrender nail clippers at the gate or just travel without them, to grin and bear it while Grandma's walker gets the once-over. (Who even remembers the relative ease of air travel pre-9/11—much less before the mid-'90s, when we first started showing picture IDs as a condition of flying?) We've already started to ignore the ubiquitous surveillance cameras like the ones that watched over us as we celebrated the Fourth of July on the Mall in Washington, D.C. We've learned to mock a never-ending series of proposals such as the infamous Operation Terrorist Information and Prevention System (TIPS) and plans for beefing up the old Neighborhood Watch program into a full-blown "national system for ... reporting suspicious activity," both of which are moving forward in modified form despite widespread hooting.

Has any of this made us safer? Not from our government, which has done little to earn our trust over the years, especially when it comes to law enforcement. And not from terrorists, either. If *they've* been cowed, it's because we went after bin Laden and his minions with specific, extreme, and righteous prejudice. It's because of regular people who took the terrorists down over Pennsylvania instead of the White House, and who wrestled shoe bomber Richard Reid onto the floor at 30,000 feet. It's because, as a nation and as individuals, we showed that we would fight for a way of life that values freedom and privacy.

How wrong, then, that we've dealt away some of our freedom and privacy for a promise of safety and security. To be sure, today's America is not [writer Jeremy] Bentham's *Panopticon* [which discusses a theme for improving prison discipline and establish an equitable legal system] or Orwell's dystopia [*1984*] (or even [Fidel] Castro's). It's not even solely a product of the September attacks, which merely hurried along trends that were already well under way. But in making the freedom-for-safety swap, we haven't just dishonored the dead of 9/11. We've helped something else die too.

Bush's Homeland Security Policies Have Not Threatened Civil Liberties

David Frum and Richard Perle

In the immediate aftermath of the September 11, 2001, terrorist attacks, the Bush administration enacted a range of laws to make it easier to track and arrest terrorists. For instance, the administration expanded the ability of law enforcement officials to "profile" or track individuals who fit certain criteria and, therefore, might be potential terrorists.

One result of these expanded law enforcement powers is that the Bush administration has been criticized for its erosion of Americans' civil liberties. Efforts to identify and apprehend potential terrorists have been perceived by groups such as the American Civil Liberties Union (ACLU) as infringements on basic rights. The ACLU contends that if terrorists force the United States to change its basic civil liberties protections, then they have in a sense won the war on terror by depriving Americans of the freedom that has defined the nation. David Frum and Richard Perle disagree with such assessments. Instead, they assert that the Bush administration's actions are reasonable and, in many instances, long overdue. Frum is a former special assistant to President George W. Bush and a resident fellow at the American Enterprise Institute. Perle is a former assistant secre-

David Frum and Richard Perle, *An End to Evil: How to Win the War on Terror*. New York: Random House, 2003. Copyright © 2003 by David Frum and Richard Perle. All rights reserved. Reproduced by permission of Random House, Inc.

tary of defense and a current resident fellow at the American Enterprise Institute.

THE PATRIOT ACT GRANTS THE FBI THE ABILITY TO CONduct twenty-first-century surveillance of terrorist suspects. It is temporary legislation—many of its provisions expire in 2005—so that Congress can return to the matter later, investigate whether abuses have taken place, and then revise the law accordingly. There's much to be said for this kind of "sunset" law. It took Congress until the mid-1970s to get around to formally terminating the state of belligerency it declared in April 1917, and World War I ended much more dramatically than the war on terrorism is likely to do.

But it was not a general wariness of obsolescence that caused the Patriot Act to be made temporary, but a very specific fear that the passions of the moment might stampede us into doing something "hysterical." Two years on, however, it is those fears of hysteria that themselves look hysterical. Civil liberties in the United States continue robust. The privacy of the American home is many millions of times more likely to be invaded by an e-mail spammer or a telemarketer than a federal agent. The right to dissent flourishes unrestrained—indeed, to judge by the way some of President Bush's wilder opponents carry on, it flourishes unrestrained even by common politeness or basic accuracy.

The Real Danger
All of this is as it should be. Yet in our appropriate zeal to preserve and defend the right to speak freely and think differently, there is a real danger that Americans will make the opposite mistake. We may be so eager to protect the right to dissent that we lose sight of the difference between dissent and subversion; so determined to defend the right of

privacy that we refuse to acknowledge even the most blatant warnings of danger.

Daniel Pipes of the Middle East Forum in Philadelphia is one of this country's most knowledgeable and rigorous experts on Islamic extremism. He recently reported the following story. In March 2003, federal agents, guns drawn, arrested an electrical engineer named Maher Mofeid "Mike" Hawash in the parking lot of the Oregon building in which he worked. Hawash, a Palestinian who had immigrated to the United States from Kuwait in 1984, was a valued employee of Intel. He earned almost $360,000 a year, had published a textbook, and was married and the father of two. Hawash's arrest and his subsequent monthlong detention ignited a firestorm of protest in the Pacific Northwest.

"One professor portrayed Hawash's incarceration as 'part of a consistent pattern of suppression of civil liberties.' Columnists and letter writers compared the United States to a 'Third World country,' Orwell's *1984*, Nazi Germany or the Soviet Union. Militant Islamic groups like the Council on American Islamic Relations [CAIR] saw in Hawash's arrest 'serious damage' to the standing of American Muslims." Hawash's friends and his immediate boss denounced the arrest as racial profiling, raised funds for a legal defense fund, set up a FreeMikeHawash.org Web site, and staged protests in the streets of Portland.

The Threat Next Door

What inspired the feds to move against Hawash? Pipes again: Sometime in the year 2000, "Hawash's neighbors began to notice a change in him. He grew a beard, wore Arab clothing, prayed five times a day and regularly attended mosque. He also became noticeably less friendly. . . . Further inquiry found that Hawash paid up his house mortgage (interest payments go against Islamic law) and donated more than $10,000 to the Global Relief Foundation, an Islamic charity subsequently closed for financing terrorist groups. Early in 2001, he went on pilgrimage to Mecca. And 'Middle Eastern males' were seen coming and going from his house."

Responding to President Bush's call for citizens to be vigilant after 9/11, Hawash's neighbors reported these strange goings-on to the FBI.

Racial profiling? On August 6, 2003, Hawash pleaded guilty to conspiring to help the Taliban and agreed to co-operate fully with the prosecution, including waiving his right to appeal his sentence. That's the kind of plea a defendant cops only when the prosecutors have him dead to rights. And the FBI might never have thought to investigate Hawash if his neighbors had not spoken up.

It's worth remembering incidents like these when you hear complaints about the Bush administration's civil liberties record. In the 2002 State of the Union address, President Bush unveiled an ambitious program that invited American workers to report suspicious activity in public places, especially docks, highways, public transit, and public utilities. These are the sorts of installations that are both most vulnerable to a destructive act of terrorism and also most difficult to police. Here's just one scenario: Ten al-Qaeda men lease ordinary-looking white trucks at ten different locations, load them with explosives, drive one into the middle of the Triborough Bridge, another onto the Golden Gate Bridge, a third to the junction of the Santa Monica and San Diego Freeways, a fourth into the center of the Chicago Loop, and so on, and then, at an appointed hour—detonate them all simultaneously. How in the world do you prevent something like that? Probably the only way would be a tip from the agent who leased one of the trucks—or else maybe a report from a keen-eyed trucker who noticed something untoward about the vehicle in the next lane. That reasonable insight was the genesis of the Terrorist Information and Prevention System, or TIPS for short. To the astonishment of the administration,

TIPS provoked an outburst of anger and mockery. Critics conjured up the possibility of deliverymen spying on their customers and meter readers peeking through the windows. The administration responded by issuing new rules that specifically exempted from the program any postal and utility employees who served or even had access to private houses. The revisions failed to mollify, and the final version of the Homeland Security Act that Bush signed in November 2002 forbade the administration to proceed with the idea.

Self-Policing

It's curious: Most of the time we praise the alert citizen who identifies and exposes wrongdoing. The actress Julia

---

Bush and Homeland Security Legislation

Barry Rubin, the deputy director of the Begin-Sadat Center for Strategic Studies, and Judith Colp Rubin, a journalist, present an overview of the homeland security legislation passed in the Bush administration.

Several new laws and regulations were enacted in the United States to deter and catch terrorists. The first executive order on September 24 [2001] was aimed at undercutting financial backing for terrorists by authorizing the seizure of the property of any individual or organization linked to terrorism. The second executive order, issued on October 8, established the Office of Homeland Security, a governmental office whose mission would be to develop, coordinate, and oversee the national fight against terrorism. The third and most controversial executive order, on November 13, called for establishing military tribunals when needed to try any non-U.S. citizens who were members of terrorist groups. The tribunals would be conducted under a different set of rules from other

---

Roberts won an Academy Award for a role based on the career of Erin Brockovich, a paralegal who accused a utility company of poisoning a community's water. White House counsel John Dean became a national icon a quarter century ago for blowing the whistle on President Nixon. Federal law affirmatively *requires* doctors, nurses, teachers, and day care workers to file a report whenever they suspect that a child has been abused. Yet many of the same people who salute the conscientious citizen who informs the authorities that she suspects a corporation may be poisoning the water would condemn her if she informed them that she suspects her tenant may be plotting to do the same.

This is all wrong. A free society is not an unpoliced society. A free society is a self-policed society. To an extent

courts, including conviction and sentencing by concurrence of two-thirds of the commission members rather than unanimously, as is the case in regular courts. Nor may defendants seek appeals in any other U.S. or international court.

On September 28 the U.S. Congress passed a major law to strengthen law enforcement efforts against terrorism, called the Uniting and Strengthening America by Providing Appropriate Tools Required to Intercept and Obstruct Terrorism, or Patriot Act. This law made it easier for law enforcement and intelligence officials to coordinate among themselves, intercept communications, block suspected foreign terrorists from entering the United States, and detain and deport those already present. It authorized the collection of information about foreigners who were in the country on student visas. A section of the bill also opposed any stigma or discrimination against Muslims, Arabs, or other groups.

Barry Rubin and Judith Colp Rubin, eds., *Anti-American Terrorism and the Middle East: A Documentary Reader.* New York: Oxford University Press, 2002, p. 318.

that often amazes people from other countries, Americans are expected to comply with the laws unsupervised. One reason that so many European countries rely so heavily on sales taxes is that they simply do not trust their people to pay their income taxes. Americans declare their income to the government, estimate their own deductions, and send a check. Americans are often called on to serve on juries. The duty is both irksome and easy to evade—yet by and large it is not evaded, and most of us are mildly scandalized when we hear that a friend or relative has tried to shirk. When we summon to memory the heroes of World War II, we think not only of the fighting men on the front line, but also of the air-raid wardens of the battle of Britain and the good citizens on the home front who donated their aluminum pots and pans to the war effort, went without tires and fresh meat, and invested every spare dollar in war bonds. We have to cast off once and for all the 1970s cynicism that sneered from the back of the classroom at the joiner and volunteer—and reacquire our admiration for the citizen who *does his or her part.* . . .

Profiling?

It would be un-American and stupid to mistrust our neighbors merely because of their names and backgrounds. The Americans of the World War II era were able to distinguish between an Eisenhower, a Wedermeyer, and a Nimitz on the one hand and a Goebbels, a Goering, and a Himmler on the other—and we are at least as capable of drawing distinctions as they were. From the Arabic speakers who translate intercepts for the National Security Agency (NSA) to the brave agents who have tried to infiltrate al-Qaeda cells; from the Afghan American taxi drivers who return home to open businesses in Kabul to intellectuals and artists like Fouad Ajami and Salman Rushdie who uphold the ideals of freedom and pluralism often at the risk of their lives—all in all, many of the most valiant and effective fighters against Islamic extremism have been men and women of Muslim faith and origin themselves. That should never be forgotten.

But neither should it be forgotten that the terrorist thrives in obscurity and inattention. Scrutiny is his deadliest enemy.

There has been much debate since 9/11 about the need for "profiling" to catch potential terrorists without forcing law-abiding travelers to stand in long lines. In our view, ethnic profiling—looking for people with Muslim-sounding names or Middle Eastern facial features—is a divisive and humiliating waste of time. As the cases of [non-Islamic terrorists] Johnny Walker Lindh, Richard Reid, and José Padilla demonstrate, Islamic terrorists can be born in any country and can belong to any race. Nor should we exclude the possibility that Islamic terrorism may begin to make common cause with Western political extremists of the far Left and the far Right. In 2002, Holland's most outspoken critic of militant Islam, Pim Fortuyn, was murdered not by a Muslim, but by a left-wing activist who (according to his own testimony) regarded Fortuyn as a "considerable danger to the weaker groups in society," which were, as the killer defined them, Muslims, asylum seekers, immigrants, and animals. Just as the communists were once aided by fellow travelers who endorsed their program and condoned their crimes, so Islamic extremists may find fellow travelers in the non-Muslim West. Indeed, they are already finding them. David Frum stood under the dome of St. Paul's Cathedral on Easter Monday 2003 and heard a minister of the Church of England preach a sermon extolling Rachel Corrie as a model of Christian courage and self-sacrifice: Corrie was the young American who was accidentally buried under a collapsing pile of dirt as she tried to block an Israeli bulldozer from excavating tunnels used to smuggle arms and explosives into Israel from Gaza. (Eleven days after Corrie's death, the Israeli Defense Forces arrested an armed Islamic

Jihad terrorist in the Jenin offices of Corrie's group, the International Solidarity Movement. ISM also hosted the British suicide bomber Asif Mohammed Hanif and his co-conspirator Omar Khan Sharif only five days before they killed three people and wounded fifty in an April 30, 2003, suicide attack on a Tel Aviv nightclub.)

Surveillance and Vigilence

What investigators need to profile is not *ethnicity*—it is *behavior*. Imagine this scenario, for example: An individual travels by air from an urban center to a rural town. He checks into a motel. He purchases a quantity of agricultural chemicals. He rents a van. He drives to another urban area, rents a storage locker, and returns the van. Then he travels by bus to New York City. Weeks later he removes the contents of the storage locker, rents another van, and drives toward New York. Yes, it is certainly possible that this individual might be an eccentric New Yorker trying to grow a lawn on the roof of his Chicago town house, who takes advantage of a visit to his cousin in Bucks County to buy chemicals at Cousin Joe's feed store. But wouldn't we like to know just a little bit more about him before we decided he was harmless?

There are new surveillance techniques that make it possible to monitor behavior indicative of terrorism without compromising the privacy of the individuals engaged in the behavior if they should later prove to be innocent. New data assembly techniques can pull together inside a computer an individual's credit history, his recent movements, his immigration status and personal background, his age and sex, and a hundred other pieces of information and present them to the analyst—*without the analyst or any other human being ever knowing the individual's identity*. The dossier of data would be assigned a case number, and stringent internal codes and controls would hermetically segregate the dossier's number from the name of the person to whom the dossier referred. Only if the dossier gave probable cause to investigate further would investigators seek a warrant to permit the name and the data to be joined together, and then to authorize further surveillance. This is profiling as it ought to be done: not an excuse for discrimination, but an attempt to concentrate scarce police resources at points of greatest danger.

Bush's Homeland Security Policies Unfairly Target Immigrants

Roberto Suro

Several of the hijackers responsible for the September 11, 2001, terrorist attacks had entered the United States on student or work visas and then remained illegally in the country. The Bush administration aimed to prevent future terrorists from operating within the United States by expanding background investigations and increasing scrutiny of immigrants and aliens attempting to enter the country. However, according to Roberto Suro in the following viewpoint, many of the new regulations have placed undue burdens on legal immigrants and aliens and have taken away their right to due process under the law. In addition, many immigrants have been arrested or questioned even though they have no links to terrorism. Suro is a former journalist and the director of the Pew Hispanic Center. He has published a variety of books on immigration in the United States.

THE TRAGEDY OF SEPTEMBER 11 IS OFTEN DEPICTED AS A fall from grace. The analogy is particularly apt in the realm of immigration policy because the attacks came at a moment of such extraordinary and rare promise. Measuring the impact of September 11 requires not only an understanding of what has happened since then but also an appreciation of what might have been:

What Might Have Been

Bush and [Mexican president Vincente] Fox were both starting their terms. They had quickly developed a personal affinity. Fox, the first Mexican president in seventy years elected from outside the Revolutionary Institutional Party, had a mandate to put aside old antagonisms in favor of new, more positive relations with the United States. Prior to entering politics, Bush had managed a business—a baseball team—heavily dependent on immigration for its talent. He came to the White House from the experience of governing Texas during a time when much of the state's business leadership embraced the new North American Free Trade Agreement as an investment and growth opportunity. He had aggressively courted Latino voters by promising, among other things, to seek a partnership with Mexico on migration issues.

Circumstances and leaders seemed ideally matched in that rare confluence that can make history. The U.S. economy's growth potential looked boundless, as did its ability to absorb ever-increasing numbers of immigrant workers without displacing natives. America's place in the world seemed generally secure, and for the most part Americans took a positive view of globalization and the nation's growing international interconnectedness. At home, relations among different races and ethnic groups had been relatively benign, at least in their outward manifestations. Nearly ten years had passed since the last major expression of intergroup violence, the Los Angeles riots of 1992. Finally, in Washington a consensus had developed in both political parties and among major interest groups that the time had come for major reform of immigration policies and the dysfunctional Immigration and Naturalization Service.

September 11 crushed the opportunity presented by that promising constellation of factors. The law enforcement regime adopted in the aftermath of the attacks has gradually come to influence more and more aspects of immigration policy. Undoubtedly one paradigm—the reform of immigration policies in the light of new economic realities—is dead or, at best, comatose. A new one—the antiterrorism paradigm—has emerged forcefully. What remains to be seen is whether these two ideas will ever have a chance to coexist.

Immigration Under Attack

Protecting the nation from potentially dangerous foreigners has been a function of the immigration system at other times of perceived threat, including the Red Scares of the 1920s and 1950s. But the national security imperative had never gained so much precedence so quickly as it has since September 11. Keeping terrorists out and tracking down those who get in could easily become defining missions for the immigration bureaucracy. That would produce a fundamental change in the purposes and character of immigration policy. However, things have not quite progressed to that point yet, at least not as of mid-2003.

Many of the new measures are ad hoc or of limited scope, and the reorganization of immigration functions into the Department of Homeland Security has only just begun. Indeed, both the system of family reunification visas, which is the largest mechanism for legal immigration, and most of the avenues for illegal entry continue to operate as before. Although the number of foreigners granted entry as immigrants has declined since September 11, many thousands continue to make their way to the United States every day. Moreover, the combination of an economic downturn and foreign terrorist attacks has yet to generate widespread expressions of anti-immigrant sentiments. No significant political leaders have tried to energize support by demonizing the foreign-born.

Indeed, there is no backlash comparable to the anti-immigrant polemics of the mid-1990s. Recall that the first World Trade Center bombing in 1993 and an economic recession combined to fuel powerful moves to restrict immigration. In 1994 California voters enacted Proposition 187, a ballot initiative that would have denied public health, education, and social services to undocumented migrants. The Republicans who took control of Congress that year proposed a variety of measures to reduce or discourage legal immigration.

Post–September 11

In the days after September 11, President Bush, New York City Mayor Rudolph Giuliani, and other prominent leaders warned loudly against a generalized anti-immigrant backlash. Most of the voices that called for wholesale cuts in immigration in the mid-1990s limited themselves to demanding tougher screening of immigrants and other such antiterrorism measures in the aftermath of the attacks.

Much has changed in the way the United States perceives and treats immigrants since September 11, but the full character and the permanence of those changes are still to be determined. The stage of emergency actions has passed, and the initial bureaucratic realignment is in place. However, many fundamental issues have yet to be broached. Whether the legacy of September 11 for immigration is a series of measures designed to make the homeland more secure or a wholesale revision of the ways the nation relates to the foreign-born is very much in play. . . .

Most of what has happened since September 11 has heightened the distinction in the civil rights accorded to citizens and noncitizens while further relying on a law enforcement approach to the screening of immigrants and visitors. Although the laws that govern the number of individuals granted entry into the country remain unchanged, the rickety balance between restriction and openness has tilted forcefully in the direction of restriction on a range of procedures involving the treatment of those individuals.

Backlash

Ten days after the September 11 attacks, Chief Immigration Judge Michael Creppy issued a memo stating that "the Attorney General has implemented additional security procedures for certain cases in the Immigration Court" that "require" all immigration judges handling such cases to "close the hearing to the public." That notification fit a pattern for what became a series of Justice Department administrative actions that curbed due process for the foreign-born in cases somehow related to what had become the war on terrorism. The notification was issued after the new rules had taken effect. Little or no explanation or rationale was offered, and there was no opportunity to challenge the action.

Around the country, federal agents picked up young men from predominately Muslim nations and detained them without pressing any charges. They were held in secret and incommunicado in prison facilities. According to a record of executive branch actions compiled by the American Immigration Lawyers Association, bond was automatically opposed with a boilerplate memo stating: "The [Federal Bureau of Investigation] is gathering and culling information that may corroborate or diminish our suspicions of the individuals who have been detained. . . . The FBI is unable to rule out the possibility that respondent is somehow linked to, or possesses knowledge of, the terrorist attacks." Despite litigation and congressional inquiries, the Justice Department kept the detainees' identities and location secret. At one point, Attorney General John Ashcroft defended his refusal to release the names of the detainees by saying, "The law properly prevents the department from creating a public blacklist of detainees that would violate their rights." The Justice Department vigorously fought off litigation and congressional inquiries that questioned whether the detentions were a gross and wholesale violation of civil rights. Eventually, the dragnet snared more than 1,000 individuals.

There was nothing new about the tactic of using the nonjudicial nature of immigration proceedings to facilitate law enforcement actions that would have been impossible with citizens, but it had never been applied in such a vast and draconian manner. The post–September 11 roundups did set a precedent of another sort, however. Repeatedly thereafter, the Justice Department aimed suspicion at broad categories of foreigners, generating an enormous workload for itself in trying to process them. The Justice Department has never offered a full accounting of the fate of the detainees. However, it appears that a handful were eventually held as material witnesses, and some more were found to be wanted for crimes unrelated to terrorism. The vast majority were held on alleged violations of their immigration status, such as overstaying a tourist visa. Dozens were held for further questioning even after their immigration cases had been resolved either with a deportation order or a voluntary departure agreement. Most of the detainees were eventually released. There are no indications that anyone caught in the autumn 2001 roundups was ever linked to the September 11 attacks or was found to possess any knowledge of them.

Casting a Wide Net

Throughout 2002 and thus far into 2003, the Justice Department has used its leverage over immigrants to cast wide nets in the hopes of catching a few potential terrorists. Initially, 5,000 young men recently arrived from nations where Al-Qaeda has a presence were called in for voluntary interviews. That program gradually expanded and eventually grew into a mandatory registration program for all males over the age of sixteen born in a swath of twenty-five Arab or Muslim countries from Pakistan to Libya. Altogether more than 30,000 individuals have been subject to various levels of scrutiny, including examination of their immigration status and a criminal background check with the National Crime Information Center database. This series of steps involved broadening circles of suspicion that encompassed larger numbers of immigrants. Starting with the detainees who had been individually targeted, the Justice Department quickly moved to a wholesale dragnet aimed at entire categories of people based on minimal criteria of age, gender, and country of origin.

Supporters of these programs argue that the effort is justified because of the extraordinary damage that a single individual can cause. Undoubtedly, eliminating a risk to thousands of lives more than outbalances inconveniencing thousands. In the wake of September 11, no one can seriously argue that the government should spare any effort if it has a chance to preempt another such attack. However, one can question whether the interview and registration programs targeted at Arab/Muslim men are an effective means of countering terrorism. Critics contend that mass screenings simply create enormous haystacks that may or may not include the proverbial needle. In this view, mass screenings are a wasteful use of resources. Moreover, critics additionally question whether Al-Qaeda operatives and their accomplices are likely to present themselves to federal authorities for registration and questioning. . . .

Changing the Process

Many of the initiatives taken since September 11 attempt to remedy the immigration system's failure to track the comings and goings of visitors and immigrants, a weakness that has been well known for more than a decade. The INS routinely reported in the 1990s that about 40 percent of the illegal alien population entered the country legally in one form or another and had simply overstayed visas. While the Clinton administration and Congress undertook an enormous buildup of border controls to block those trying to enter the country without authorization, no parallel action was aimed at these so-called overstayers. The lack of urgency stemmed at least in part from the fact that although they represent a large share of the unauthorized population, overstayers are a tiny fraction of the massive flow of visitors. The first World Trade Center bombing drew attention to the problem when investigators learned that several of the alleged plotters and accomplices had entered the country legally and overstayed. In response, Congress, in the ostentatiously named Illegal Immigration Reform and Immigrant Responsibility Act of 1996, required the INS to begin developing means to track overstayers—but set long lead times for compliance. Needless to say, no systems were in place on September 11, when the attacks suddenly made the issue an emergency matter. As with so much else, what had been just one other concern in the clunky, often haphazard process of developing immigration policies and procedures now came under the aegis of the war on terrorism.

The Entry-Exit Program mandated by Congress in 1996 is supposed to record data on all temporary foreign visitors as they arrive in the country and maintain the information in an automated system enabling immigration authorities to instantly determine whether an individual has overstayed his visa. Starting with airports, the system is supposed to be put in place at all ports of entry between 2003 and the end of 2005. In the meantime, however, the Justice Department, by administrative decree, is rushing into place the National Security Entry-Exit Registration System, which will gather detailed information on visitors "coming from certain countries or who meet a combination of intelligence-based criteria and are identified as presenting elevated national security concerns," according to a Justice Department news release.

In this case, however, the change in the substance and the tenor of immigration policy goes far beyond what has become the suspect class of Arab or Muslim nationalities. In post–September 11 legislation, Congress sped up and significantly toughened plans for the Student and Exchange Visitor Information System, which had been in place since 1996. Since January 1, 2003, for example, schools are required to notify the authorities if an individual on a student visa fails to register within thirty days of his expected arrival and must provide updated information on any changes in a student's address, course load, or field of study. Failure to meet strict reporting deadlines can jeopardize a school's certification for the enrollment of foreign students. Approximately 1 million people in a constantly changing flux will be covered by the new regulations at any one time, according to the Justice Department.

Catch-22

More broadly still, the Justice Department promulgated a regulation in July 2002 that requires any alien—a legal permanent resident or a visitor—to register a change of address within ten days. Ostensibly, this simply enforced a provision of immigration law that had been on the books for fifty years but that had been ignored by the authorities for so long that the proper forms for filing an address change were unavailable at most INS offices.

In addition, however, the Justice Department added what amounts to a classic Catch-22. That regulation requires every alien to acknowledge receipt of a notice that he or she is obliged to provide a valid address. Such notice can be mailed to the alien's last known address. If the alien does not respond, he or she is automatically considered guilty of a "willful" failure to comply, which can produce criminal prosecution or a deportation order issued in absentia. Of course, if the alien has moved from the last address registered with the Justice Department or is simply traveling for a time, he or she will not receive the notice. Thus, a legal immigrant of long standing could leave the country on vacation and, upon returning, find himself detained at the airport and put in secret deportation proceedings without the right to counsel, appeal, or even a phone call. Presumably, this sort of device could make it very easy to snare someone suspected of some involvement with a terrorist group. But then again, the Justice Department has already demonstrated that it considers itself authorized to detain and hold any alien on the grounds of such suspicions alone.

The United States was long overdue for a program that would identify foreign visitors who overstay or otherwise abuse their visas, and such an effort might even have proved to be an effective device for reducing the undocumented population if it were part of a broader, systemic reform of immigration policies and procedures. Overstaying visas has become an increasingly attractive means of residing in the United States because so much else in the immigration system is broken. Backlogs for many categories of family reunification visas that permit permanent legal residency have grown so long that coming to the United States as a visitor, and remaining illegally with relatives until the green card clears, has become an increasingly popular tactic. Indeed, immigration law tacitly acknowledges this practice by allowing the issuance of green cards to thousands of people every year who are already residing here illegally. Many of the Arab or Muslim men deported for violations of immigration status after getting caught up in the mass screenings were simply playing the game according to rules that the federal government has long acknowledged by way of winks and nods.

CHAPTER
3

THE ECONOMY

Bush's Economic Plan Can Steer the Economy to Recovery

Richard Nadler and Dan Perrin

Under Bush, the federal deficit has increased dramatically. However, in the following essay Richard Nadler and Dan Perrin defend Bush's management of the economy. They argue that much of the spending has been due to increases in defense expenditures necessary to wage the war on terror and protect homeland security. In addition, Bush's tax cuts have spurred economic growth, they believe. Finally, the authors contend that reform of entitlement programs, while costly, will control future spending and provide long-term savings. Richard Nadler is the political director of the Republican Leadership Coalition, a Washington-based independent political organization that promotes conservative governance. Dan Perrin is the executive director of the Republican Leadership Coalition.

N O ONE DOUBTS THAT PRESIDENT GEORGE W. BUSH INherited what Office of Management and Budget Director Josh Bolten calls "a perfect storm"—an imploding market punctuated by a symptomatic series of corporate scandals, exacerbated by a costly terrorist assault on American soil.

Richard Nadler and Dan Perrin, "Q: Can Republicans Really Be Trusted to Stem Runaway Spending in 2004? YES: The GOP Budget Plan Is Steering the Nation and the Economy Out of the 'Perfect Storm,'" *Insight on the News*, February 2, 2004, pp. 46–49. Copyright © 2004 by News World Communications. All rights reserved. Reproduced by permission.

The Deficit, in Perspective

The deficit magnitudes are not in question. The shortfall for the fiscal year ending Sept. 30, 2003, was $374 billion. The projected deficit for fiscal 2004 may exceed $500 billion. It is how the president addresses this imbalance that draws fire, left and right. While attacking the spending side, these critics pay little heed to the transformational changes that accompanied them in national security, entitlement reform and economic efficiency.

The deficit, a product of multiple crises, is surely steep. But it is below its historic peaks. The shortfall equaled 3.5 percent of gross domestic product (GDP) in fiscal 2003 and may reach 4.5 percent of GDP in fiscal 2004. By contrast, Reagan-era deficits reached 6 percent of GDP.

Bolten observes that spending growth unrelated to national security has declined consistently relative to the 15 percent increase in the final Clinton budget to 6 percent in fiscal 2002, 5 percent in fiscal 2003 and no more than 4 percent in fiscal 2004.

But the debate over the Bush budget concerns its magnitude less than its tendency. From 2001 to 2003, the federal budget increased $296 billion. Roughly 34 percent of this increase went to defense; another 11 percent to homeland security. But entitlement outlays accounted for most of the rest: roughly 15 percent for Social Security, 9 percent for Medicare and 14 percent for Medicaid. The combined impact of these programs—defense, homeland security, Social Security and medical care—thus encompassed 83 percent of the total budget increase.

Defense

The deficit means different things to its different critics: an indictment of defense costs or tax cuts to those on the left; an indictment of spending, particularly of entitlement growth, to those on the right.

Let's start with the military budget. The $87 billion supplemental request shocked only those who didn't understand the stakes involved. The low-tech, mass homicides of 9/11 cost this country roughly $150 billion in reduced GDP. Testifying before the Senate Appropriations Committee, Defense Secretary Donald Rumsfeld recently listed some of the damages incurred: $50 billion in costs to the insurance industry; $33 billion in private-sector security expenses; $21 billion to New York City for direct damages; $18 billion in cleanup costs at the World Trade Center site; $11 billion in lost business to the airline industry; $7.8 billion in lost income for the families of the roughly 3,000 murdered victims; $6.4 billion in lost wages for nonvictim New York City workers; $4 billion to the victims' compensation fund; $1.3 billion by state governments for homeland security; and $700 million to repair the Pentagon.

The capitalist order depends on a baseline of respect for persons and property—"Thou shalt not kill" and "Thou shalt not steal." Terrorism on the scale of 9/11 threatens that order's existence. Through such acts terrorists could manipulate capital markets to finance their future activities. Creative destruction, the hallmark of market economies, would be replaced by cancerous destruction.

President Bush undertook the effective response that was available: to disincent the terrorist enterprise. That meant killing the terrorists in their persons while placing a military presence at the throat, or in the face, of their state sponsors. Thus far the dividends have surpassed expectations: mass terror extinct on U.S. soil and a chain-reaction change of heart among state sponsors of such acts. Given what was at stake, the budgetary "price" was cheap.

Taxes

The second controversial expenditure of the Bush budget is visible only to critics on the left—i.e., "tax expenditures" in the form of lower marginal rates, investment tax credits, child credits, and reductions on the taxation of inheritance, capital gains, dividends and other forms of saving. It was a bold move by President Bush to lower taxes in the face of the "perfect storm" raging about the budget, but the results have been gratifying. GDP growth hit a sizzling 8.2 percent in the third quarter of 2003, spurred by revivals in manufacturing, foreign trade, retail sales, housing construction and, finally, employment.

It is not our intention to justify every domestic expenditure of the Bush budget. But it is fair to state that where he has accepted major domestic-spending increases, he has balanced them with structural reforms that will move the budget back toward balance in the future.

Health Care

Let's look at the Medicare prescription-drug bill just passed [in 2003]. The president and the Republican Congress fulfilled a promise that they have been making to America's seniors year after year: Medicare should have a prescription-drug option.

The reforms contained in this legislation were substantially greater than anything that could have passed Congress as stand-alone measures. These included tax-sheltered, personally controlled health-savings accounts (HSAs) for everyone, and a huge pilot project for privatizing Medicare involving 8 million to 10 million seniors.

The health-care-cost crisis plaguing the private sector in the United States is so acute that small businesses and large companies use the word "unsustainable" to describe it. In fact, the chief executive officer of Wal-Mart recently said it was time for the "government to step in" on health care.

Why would a Wal-Mart executive prefer socialized medicine to the current health-benefits environment? Answer: Business is being hammered relentlessly by health-care costs.

Here are some sobering numbers. In 2003, the average cost of health insurance for a family was $9,068 per year, and health-insurance costs are expected to rise by at least 10 percent this year. A 12 percent increase would mean health costs have doubled since 1999. The employer-provided health-insurance base is shrinking. It now is at 45 percent, down from 63 percent 10 years ago. At the current rate of decline, only 36 percent of the population will have employer-provided health insurance five years hence.

All conservatives know that HSAs, tax sheltered and individually controlled, are the sole practical market reform that can derail the march to socialized medicine and its inevitable service declines, cost inefficiencies and treatment quotas. A *Reason* magazine article titled "Health Insurance Crisis Again" recently explained that "such plans typically cost 20 percent to 60 percent less than conventional health-insurance policies." As Newt Gingrich recently wrote in *Saving Lives & Saving Money*, HSA-style accounts will enable everyone to "become the primary guardian of how money is spent on health care. No longer beholden to insurance companies' regulations, doctors will be driven by market forces to provide better care at lower cost."

The 60-vote hurdle necessary to move legislation in the Senate is insurmountable unless some Democrats vote with Republicans—i.e., they get something they want, so we get something we want. But failure to pass the president's prescription-drug package would have relegated the only practical mechanism we have to control health-care costs to think-tank forums, where some of our friends seem to want it.

Critics of the right savage this proposal on the basis of the prescription-drug benefit that accompanied it. But without the transformational power of a direct consumer market in health care, it is hard to see how the burgeoning cost of Medicare can be contained.

It also should be noted that hundreds of billions of dollars in HSAs will build up over the next five to 10 years, providing a working model for Social Security privatization—

a point that Sen. Ted Kennedy (D-Mass.) made repeatedly in his filibuster of HSAs and the Medicare prescription-drug bill.

Reform

The Bush tax cuts contained other generous provisions for savers and investors, and the 2004 budget may contain more. If capital markets prove vigorous in 2004, we may see the centerpiece of the Bush entitlement-reform agenda: personal retirement accounts within the Social Security system. The bipartisan President's Commission to Strengthen Social Security (2001) designed three workable models for such accounts. The partial conversion of Social Security tax into personal savings, fully inheritable, accumulating at market rates, is the last, best chance to improve retirement security while avoiding a budget crisis.

Absent such sweeping reform, it is likely that the 2004 budget will include other incentives for savers and investors a supplementary retirement-savings account and/or a "universal" IRA for a variety of life-cycle needs, such as education, home ownership and health care.

The Bush Revolution

To summarize, the Bush administration approach to entitlement reform is to substitute personal, tax-advantaged savings and investments for a portion of the traditional "safety net," creating higher rates of accumulation and return on the one hand, and a competitive benchmark for the public sector on the other.

President Ronald Reagan's supply-side tax cuts turned the United States into a haven for capital. His 401(k) revolution turned the American laborer into a worker-capitalist, an owner of financial assets. And his defense buildup won the Cold War. In the process, he threw the federal budget into deficit. But the structural changes he effected transformed not only the economy, but the electorate. The taming of inflation in the 1980s, and the balancing of the budget in the 1990s, were direct consequences of the new economy and the new labor market.

Today, President Bush is undertaking a comparable revolution. His war against terror sustains the capitalist order; his tax cuts magnify it. His transformation of entitlements forces market incentives on the nation's most hegemonic bureaucracies, making Americans the masters of their own health care, retirement and education. To the extent that the president's reforms take root, the budget deficits accompanying them will be remembered no more than those of his illustrious predecessor.

Bush's Economic Strategy Will Create a Long-Term Crisis

Allen Schick

Bush became president as the "baby boom" generation began to retire. This large mass of Americans will need significant expenditures from Social Security and Medicare over the next several decades. However, Allen Schick asserts in the following selection that just as the federal government will need additional resources to aid the baby boomers, Bush has depleted resources through tax cuts and increased expenditures, thus creating a major deficit. Schick argues that Bush intentionally did this to force the federal government to limit new programs and limit future growth. The author believes this is a shortsighted strategy. He claims that it will create a crisis in the near future because government resources will not be able to meet the demands of the population. Allen Schick, an expert on the budget and public policy, is a visiting fellow at the Brookings Institute and the author of several books on economic and budget policy.

IT WAS GEORGE W. BUSH'S MISFORTUNE TO BECOME PRESI-dent just about the time the stock market bubble burst, the economy weakened, and federal revenues plummeted. It will be his successor's misfortune to enter office with an inadequate revenue base and an urgent need to push a tax increase through Congress. But even if the next president reverses course on budget policy, the aftereffects of Bush's government-by-deficit strategy will linger for many years.

Assuming he wins a second term, Bush will be the last president before the front edge of the baby boom generation reaches retirement age. His successor will have to deal with the economic and budgetary implications of an aging U.S. population in ways that Bush has not. The future financing of Social Security and Medicare is not the only problem the current president has slighted; he also has not faced up to the escalating costs of national defense and homeland security. During the first decade of the new century, the security costs added by Bush are likely to exceed the $1.3 trillion his 2001 tax cut subtracted from federal revenues. Less than two years after this tax cut, while the United States was at war in Iraq, Bush pressured Congress to enact another trillion-dollar tax cut that was estimated to reduce federal revenues by $330 billion, but whose full cost may be more than double that amount. When the books are closed on his presidency, a country that at the beginning of the century was moving to liquidate the $3.7 trillion in federal debt held by the public will instead add $1 trillion to $3 trillion to its debt burden. Which end of that range materializes will depend more on the length of Bush's stay in office than on the performance of the economy.

A Recipe for Deficit

It is easy to tar Bush as fiscally irresponsible, as Democratic leaders and a few rank-and-file Republicans have. The same week that warfare broke out in Iraq [in March 2003], key presidential aides were pressuring ambivalent Republicans in Congress to vote for a budget resolution that ensured passage of his second round of mega-tax cuts in 2003. Bush is the first president in American history to combine a call to arms and a significant tax reduction in the same political package. By some bad-, not worst-case scenarios, Bush's recipe will produce deficits in the vicinity of $500 billion a year, almost double the previous record, set by his father.

How did this president lose his way on fiscal prudence? Why did he not use September 11 to rally support for taxes to finance homeland and national security? Arguably, had he done so Bush might have been in a stronger position to ward off spending demands from Congress, including many from fellow Republicans. It may be that Bush miscalculated, that he did not know that the budget would spin out of control, and that faced with a rush of bad news—a weak economy, spiraling defense costs, and plummeting revenues—he let things drift in the expectation that conditions would improve if he stayed the course. When they did not, he was left with a record budget deficit that could not be trimmed through politically acceptable options. In characterizing George W. Bush's thinking, I mean to spell out the logic of the positions he takes, not to purport to psychoanalyze him.

A Colossal Misstep

Yet miscalculation does not fit this calculating president who, in contrast to his father, knows how to use the power of the office. This is a president who has not fought for a lot of things he professes to want—Medicare prescription drug coverage, abortion restrictions, and Social Security reform, to name some of his most prominent aims—but he has twice fought for big tax cuts. This is a president whose eyes are wide open to the short- and long-term fiscal and policy implications of the revenue losses he has imposed on the federal government. Even as he has truncated the budget horizon from ten years to five, he has been aware of the doomsday projections that if current policy, continues, a generation from now Social Security and Medicare will claim almost all of the federal revenue, leaving very little for the rest of government. He wants to strip the government of future revenue, not in spite of these dire scenarios but because of them. He sees revenue privation as the only or best weapon to change the course of budgetary history, a history that for him probably began with Reagan's victory in 1980. Bush is an avid student of recent political failures, in particular his father's failed presidency and the failure of both Reagan and his father to halt the expansion of government. George W. Bush wants a smaller government, and he is willing to pay the budgetary price to get it. In contrast to Reagan, he has not launched a rhetorical challenge to big government, preferring instead to let budgetary realities do the job for him. In contrast to his father, George W. Bush is not willing to let adverse budgetary numbers get in the way of his determination to purge the government of revenue. The elder Bush said, "Read my lips, no new taxes" and signed a large tax increase into law. The younger Bush does not want to repeat his father's backpedaling. In contrast to both Reagan and his father, Bush has had a Republican Congress through most of his first term, making it much easier to muscle his tax cuts through the House and Senate.

At times the White House trots out its version of the "It's the economy" defense to argue that the deficit has been the product of an economic force majeure, that the rising tide of red ink has been caused by the plunging stock market and the fragile economy, not by policy changes. This "no-fault" defense does not square with the facts, however. Critical turning points in budgeting—from deficits to surpluses in the 1990s and back to deficits in the present decade—did not just happen; they were driven in substantial part by changes in federal revenue or spending policy. For Bush no less than for his predecessors, policy matters in budgeting. Moreover, policy mistakes—and I consider the current fiscal posture a colossal misstep—take a long time to wash out of the federal budget. It took the federal government twenty-eight years (from 1970 to 1998) to produce a surplus, but only four years to return to a deficit. The symmetry in budget cycles is due to policy biases, not economic swings. It is far easier for politicians to cut taxes than to raise them, and far easier to boost spending than to curtail it. Economic weakness impels the government to spend more than it takes in; economic strength also impels it to spend more, though not necessarily more than the revenue it produces. At this point, no one knows whether the nation will go through another twenty-eight-year spell of deficits, but it is not too early to predict that the government will not be able to liquidate annual deficits if it stays on the current budget course.

Depleting Government Resources

Bush is a president who has learned from the recent past and is looking to change the future, and he is willing to risk the present to accomplish his aims. He has been told that discretionary spending will go up a lot more than his official forecast shows, that his proposal to allocate $400 billion for Medicare prescription drug coverage will not suffice, that in the next decade Social Security surpluses will diminish, and that before 2020 Medicare will be insolvent. He knows that spending on homeland security and national defense will soar tens of billions above budgeted levels and that the new Bush doctrine of preemptive war will be costly. But instead of conceding the need for a more robust revenue base, Bush firmly believes that only a vastly larger, perhaps unmanageable, deficit can curb the relentless expansion of government.

Thus the Bush White House is not clueless on the fiscal course the president has charted; this is not a case of ignorance aforethought. The administration knows what it wants and is setting out to get it. Bush's revenue policy is actually a spending strategy. He wants revenue deprivation to force a truly fundamental change in the course of government. Rather than tinker with Social Security and Medicare so that they can muddle through a few more decades, Bush wants the government to be so depleted of resources that it cannot come to their rescue. Rather than fight and lose on appropriation bills, Bush wants Congress to come to its own realization that the spending culture of Capitol Hill has to be purged. . . .

Spending Cuts

As a president who wants to reduce the size of government, George W. Bush is reticent about where most of the cuts will fall. In contrast to his father and Ronald Reagan, who listed many of the programs that were to be terminated or curtailed, this president veils his cuts in projections that show appropriations rising about as fast as inflation during his hoped-for two-term administration, and he promises new money for Medicare and some other entitlement programs. One must plumb the budget's accounts to find the many programs that will grow less than inflation or that will lose resources through various reforms. Few of the cutbacks are so dramatic as to provoke the "dead on arrival" verdict that accompanied the budgets of his Republican predecessors. If Bush has his way, during his presidency many programs will be scaled back simply because there will not be enough money to go around, not because he has launched a frontal attack on government. . . .

Budget conservatives view the trends as confirming runaway government expansion. In fiscal 1965, the last year before the Vietnam War build-up, defense appropriations were more than double those for all domestic programs. By 2000, however, domestic appropriations exceeded defense spending. Much of this shift in relative spending occurred in the 1990s, after the cold war ended but before September 11 triggered a new upsurge in defense spending. Defense poses a dilemma for Bush in working toward his objective of shrinking the size of government; in thinking that the federal government has grown too large, he clearly has domestic programs in mind, but he knows that defense spending opens the door to more domestic spending, first, by building support for tax increases, and second, by increasing overall appropriations, creating a situation in which domestic spending can displace defense appropriations when the threat to national security recedes. This "displacement effect" is one of the leading factors explaining government expansion in democratic countries, and it has been a recurring pattern in American budgetary history. If past trends continue, the surge in defense spending during the Bush administration will facilitate a big expansion in domestic programs sometime in the future. To ward this off, Bush is not paying for additional defense spending with tax increases, as was the case in most past military engagements. Moreover, he has been somewhat tight-fisted in supplementing defense appropriations, resisting demands from military leaders for more resources. In fact, Bush has augmented the defense budget much less than Reagan, to whom he is sometimes compared, did two decades ago. Reagan boosted defense spending from 4.9 percent of GDP in 1980 to a peak of 6.2 percent in 1986; the Bush scenario (which excludes the war in Iraq) projects defense outlays' declining from 3.5 percent of GDP in 2003 to 3.3 percent five years later. Perhaps Bush is a skinflint who dislikes spending any money, or perhaps he has been indoctrinated by Vice President [Dick] Cheney and Secretary of Defense [Donald] Rumsfeld in the view that the best way to get military leaders to restructure the armed forces is to squeeze them on money. But it also is likely that Bush is wary of pumping up defense too fast lest Congress siphon off some of the money for domestic priorities.

This pattern is clearly evident with regard to homeland security, Bush's most prominent government initiative. Immediately after September 11, in both regular and supplemental appropriations bills, Bush strongly opposed efforts by congressional Democrats and some Republicans to provide more money for "first responders" and other state and local security-related activities. At first glance, it seems it would have been an easy call for Bush to give state and local governments enough to at least reimburse their out-of-pocket security costs. Bush, however, clearly saw this as a domestic spending issue; he was convinced that giving states and localities money labeled "homeland security" would enable them to spend more on ongoing activities that would have little to do with making the nation more secure.

Bush's parsimony has surprised some who expected his experience as governor of Texas to sensitize him to the fiscal plight of many states whose budgets have been severely imbalanced by the economic downturn and other adversities. His failure to help the states has welled out of an overriding concern: that added expenditure would enlarge both the federal budget and the budgets of state governments. The president views state deficits the same way he views the new federal deficit, as opportunities for the states to curtail spending. If they do not, it is their problem, not the federal government's. . . .

The Outcome

As a student of recent political history, Bush has been most influenced by spending patterns during the three presidencies that immediately preceded his. Reagan succeeded in downsizing real discretionary spending, principally through blitzkrieg victories during his first year in office. But Reagan's successes were not lasting, and by 1996, less than a decade after he retired, real spending was above the level he had inherited at the start of his presidency. How and why did this happen? Bush and fellow conservatives are certain that the large tax increases enacted in 1990 and 1993 fueled the regrowth of government. Rather than paying down the deficit, which is the way economists generally view the tax increases, conservatives argue that they opened the door to bigger government.

The Bush Deficit Was Unavoidable and Harmless

David Gelernter

Many commentators who criticize Bush's handling of the economy cite the growing budget deficit during his presidency and point out that under his predecessor, Bill Clinton, the budget ran a surplus. However, in the following selection, David Gelernter maintains that the deficit under Bush was the inevitable result of the faltering economy he inherited and the necessary spending in the war on terrorism. Moreover, according to Gelernter, the deficit will most likely have no harmful long-term consequences. Gelernter is a professor of computer science at Yale University and a contributing editor to the *Weekly Standard*, a conservative weekly journal.

━━━━━━━━━━

SOME PEOPLE WANT TO KNOW, HOW CAN THE BUSH ADministration commit the moral perfidy of first squandering the Clinton budget surplus, then running up huge deficits that the "next generation" will have to pay for?

The assumptions beneath this question are all wrong. The looming deficit might or might not be important, but it has no moral implications of any kind. As for the economy, the president's performance has not been perfect, but he's done fine under the circumstances. The mistakes he has made would have been hard for any president to avoid.

It would be nice if the deficit were smaller. Then again, borrowing money is, at base, a bet that you will be richer in the future than you are today. Will this nation continue—allowing for regular business-cycle fluctuations—to grow richer? We don't really know, anything could happen, who can say, no one can predict—waffle, waffle, waffle—and the answer is yes. So, it's hard to get too worked up over the deficit. Most Americans agree. Anyone who thinks that the deficit is hot news in the sushi bars and Thai restaurants of Middle America has not been paying attention.

Facts on the ground: The president inherited a collapsing economy. (The recession kicked in seven weeks after President Bush succeeded Bill Clinton.) Then came Sept. 11, 2001, war in Afghanistan, war in Iraq and consequent huge increases in military and security-related spending. Meanwhile, the president cut taxes and increased domestic spending. Lower taxes were a reasonable response to a slow economy. Higher military spending was the only possible response to 9/11. Together, they produced a fiscal climate that was bound to cause deficit problems.

Today the deficit and the economy have both roared back. This year's [2003] deficit might be something like $500 billion. The quarter ending in September saw the fastest economic growth in 20 years; job creation also seems to be picking up.

The Basic Nature of Deficits

Let's look at the basic nature of deficits. (Don't worry, I'm no economist.) Some people say the administration, by running up the national debt, is saddling "our children" with our expenses. But if I take out a 20-year mortgage on my house, that doesn't mean I'm inflicting my debts on my children or the "next generation." Nor does it mean (although many people would once have interpreted it to mean) that morally I am a weak character. Borrowing money is a practical decision with no intrinsic moral implications.

Deficits and household mortgages are not the same. Neither are they wholly different. Twenty years from now, the adult population of America will be mostly the same as it is today. Granted, when a nation borrows, some of the eventual payers-off will not have been around when the original charges were incurred. But that doesn't mean they won't benefit from the long-ago loan. Had we chosen not to overthrow tyrants in Afghanistan and Iraq, the deficit would almost certainly be no big deal today. Overthrowing tyrants is a gift that keeps giving. Howard Dean's[1] grandchildren will bless George W. Bush. And if future generations wind up paying part of the tab, I doubt they will whine. More likely they will thank us, and write books about what a great generation we were.

Bush could have tried to cut discretionary domestic spending, and hasn't. Instead, he has signed lots of pork into law and wants to sign more. That's the American way. It's not a part of the American way I'm proud of, but I don't know how to fix it. Somehow I'm not absolutely certain the Democrats do either. If they have a solution, let's hear it.

Yet suppose that, some time over the last few years, Congress had reared up on its hind trotters and announced: We must cut spending, or cancel some tax cuts, or raise taxes in some other way, because otherwise deficits are going to the moon. Most likely the American public would have yawned—and would have added, by way of explanation: "Listen. On a percentage-of-GDP basis, we're looking at deficits that might rival what we saw in 1983, the worst deficit year since the end of World War II. But what followed 1983? A strong and sustained economic boom, and in percentage terms, lower deficits. So, what's your problem?"

---

1. Dean was a Democratic presidential candidate in 2003–2004.

The Basics Are OK

Is the deficit unacceptably high? The richer you are, the higher percentage of income you can afford to pay in taxes. A related principle probably holds for nations: The richer they are, the higher the percentage of debt they can heft without hurting themselves. A "moderate," "manageable" deficit is easy to define: one that doesn't damage the basic soundness of the economy. One that doesn't shake people's or other nations' willingness to take a chance on this country by lending it money, putting money into its ventures and investing their lives in its future. Under this theory, if interest rates are moderate (and they are) and investment rates are decent (and they are) and the net flow of manpower and brainpower is in and not out (as it is), then the basics are OK. We can expect interest rates to rise some, with the deficit. We can live with that.

And what about that famous Clinton surplus, that "legacy" we have blown? Legacy, hell. A federal government that is running a surplus is holding us up, strong-arming the nation. Suppose you were in the habit of handing someone money to buy you pizza. If you handed him too much ("Here's $20, get me a medium with mushrooms"), you'd expect him to hand you the change back. Should he announce casually one evening, "By the way, I'm running a surplus," you might want to know why. Should he explain that he's got a few thousand of your dollars in his back pocket, having decided (in his wisdom) to set them aside for you instead of returning them, lest you blow the money on something stupid instead of more pizza . . . he'd be out of a job.

The federal government is our agent. We give it tax money so it can operate the nation. If we hand it too much and it keeps the change instead of returning it—runs a surplus, builds a national "legacy"—it is acting like an officious, well-meaning crook. This is what John O'Sullivan, former editor of *National Review*, calls "Olympian" liberal-ism. We never asked the government to please hold some of our money lest we run out and waste it. It is ours to waste. On moral grounds, budget surpluses are far more likely to pose problems than deficits.

Nowadays, whenever we see Democratic caucus or primary campaigns on TV, we seem always to have tuned in the Bugs Bunny version by accident. You expect each distinguished candidate in turn to step up to the mike and launch a furious attack on the president that soars higher and higher into the pristine upper reaches of rage until he goes straight into orbit (shaking his fists and sputtering) and is never heard from again. (Next candidate, please?)

But on the deficit issue we get a break, and we deserve one. There is nothing ignoble or intrinsically wrong in the Democratic idea that we should raise our taxes for the long-term good of the nation. But worrying about the long-term consequences of today's economic decisions is like worrying about the long-term consequences of spitting into the Atlantic. Yes, there are consequences, but ultimately they depend on all sorts of things that have yet to happen, and we are in no position to calculate them. I am not opposed to long-term economic planning; it's just that history makes clear that there is no such thing.

CHAPTER

4

DOMESTIC
ISSUES AND THE
ENVIRONMENT

Bush Forged Bipartisan Consensus on Education

Siobhan Gorman

One of the early political successes of the Bush administration was the passage of an education law in 2002 that called for annual testing in reading and math for schoolchildren in grades three through eight and new measures to identify and help schools that failed to adequately educate children. In the following selection, Siobhan Gorman gives credit to Bush for arranging bipartisan support for the bill but notes that many compromises had to be made to gain broad support. These compromises, including dropping provisions aimed at increasing school accountability, undermined the overall goals of the bill. In addition, Gorman notes that the bill also needs stronger enforcement measures; past educational initiatives have often fallen short of their goals because of a lack of enforcement by the federal and state governments. Siobhan Gorman is a reporter who covers education and educational policy for the *National Journal*.

A MID A THRONG OF CHEERING TEENAGERS IN THE HAMIL-ton High School gymnasium, President Bush declared victory. "Today begins a new era, a new time in public education in our country," he intoned confidently into the microphone. "As of this hour, America's schools will be on a new path of reform, and a new path of results." With that, he signed into law the bill that reflected much of his education agenda. This Ohio school was the first stop of the two day tour the president and his merry band of liberal and conservative lawmakers took in January [2002] to celebrate the president's first true bipartisan triumph.

The Tough Road Ahead

But the party's a bit premature. To be sure, the president gets credit for forging a consensus after years of ideological and political gridlock. And the law does make some significant changes in federal education policy. Nevertheless, the reauthorized Elementary and Secondary Education Act (ESEA) hardly represents a new era. Instead, it builds on at least a decade's worth of federal reform efforts. Where the Bush administration could make its mark is in its enforcement of the law, an area in which few, if any, previous administrations have found the political will to play rough with the states.

The law calls for annual tests in reading and math for children in grades 3 through 8, plus a science test in three different grade levels by the 2007–08 school year. (States were already required to test students once in high school.) States must also establish a definition of a failing school that meets federal guidelines. Schools labeled failing for two or more years face increasingly stringent penalties, which states must impose. The law also leaves a host of issues unresolved, giving the states and the federal Department of Education plenty of wiggle room. Thus the quality of implementation may vary widely.

The federal government sports a sobering track record when it comes to enforcing its education reforms. President Clinton's 1994 ESEA reauthorization was hailed by proponents as "the most extensive revision of the legislation since [its enactment in] 1965." It required the states to develop standards and assessments linked to the standards. But lawmakers like Representative George Miller, D-Cal., say the changes envisioned by the 1994 reauthorization didn't live up to their billing because "its implementation was fudged by the administration."

Lawmakers in both parties hope that this time a combination of tough federal sanctions, more public reporting of student performance, and an aggressive White House will be enough to prompt change in the schoolhouse. This bill delivers the goals and the tools to achieve them, says Miller, one of the four top congressional negotiators on the bill. Still, he says, "The bill is not a silver bullet."...

Bipartisanship

Once elected, President Bush sent the early message that he wanted an education bill, and he wanted it to be a bipartisan one. Before his inauguration, Bush held a bipartisan education meeting in Austin, and among the hand-picked Democrats attending was Sen. Evan Bayh, D-Ind. Bayh and Sen. Joseph I. Lieberman, D-Conn., had put forth an education reform bill in early 2000 called the Three R's, aimed at bridging the partisan divide in education.

Borrowing liberally from Lieberman and Bayh's reform package, Bush said that the 54 federal elementary and secondary education programs should be consolidated into five categories reflecting federal priorities: 1) educating disadvantaged students; 2) teacher quality; 3) English fluency; 4) school choice; and 5) school safety. Bush also proposed that states begin testing children in grades 3 through 8. He wanted to allow children in schools that failed to close the achievement gap for three straight years to use federal money to attend private schools. On his second full day in office, Bush unveiled an education "blueprint" that was essentially the same as his campaign proposal. The White House immediately began negotiating with the 10 centrist Democrats cosponsoring the Lieberman-Bayh bill, which they reintroduced the day Bush unveiled his proposal, in an effort to cut a deal quickly.

However, when it became clear by the spring that Bush's tax cut would pass with the help of a few centrist Democrats, the Lieberman-Bayh group became leery of ditching their party a second time. The White House had also begun negotiating with Sen. Edward M. Kennedy, D-Mass., and the centrist Democrats feared that the White House would play the centrist and liberal Democrats against one another. For instance, the White House got Kennedy to agree to a limited voucher to pay for tutoring services. It then took that agreement to the New Democrats, who had been holding out on a voucher compromise, to try to get the New Democrats to incorporate the tutoring proposal into the deal they were negotiating separately with the White House. To avoid this, Lieberman decided that future negotiations would have to include Kennedy.

A new negotiating group formed, this time including the White House, Republicans, New Democrats, and Kennedy sympathizers. After a month of negotiations, the group reached agreement on the two most controversial issues: vouchers and block grants. They went with Kennedy's voucher compromise, which allowed students in failing schools to use federal money for private tutoring. They also agreed to a scaled-back block-grant proposal that would have allowed 7 states and 25 school districts to sign a performance contract with the federal government that would free them of most federal education regulations in exchange for a promise to improve student performance. They thought they had a bill ready to send to the Senate floor.

Enter Politics

But at a late-night meeting in mid-April, one congressional aide announced that 80 to 90 percent of the schools in states like Texas and North Carolina, both of which had seen rising achievement scores through the 1990s, would be deemed "falling" under the bill's definition. The bill required states to set performance goals for every demo-graphic group of students. The problem was that if a school didn't meet that goal for any one group in any grade level in any one year, it would be labeled failing.

Two weeks later, the senators settled on a complicated formula that required states to calculate an overall perfor-mance grade for a school based on several factors, includ-ing improving test scores for poor and minority children. But no longer could a school receive a failing grade solely because its poor and minority students didn't see their test scores rise. By the time this definition was devised, it was early May. The Senate began debate, but it dragged on for six weeks as the Senate juggled campaign finance reform and turned over to Democratic control.

On the House side, the bill moved more quickly. A series of bipartisan negotiations between Reps. Miller and John Boehner, R-Ohio, chairman of the House Committee on

---

Sensible Ideas for Schools

The Economist *magazine suggests that his education bill reveals Bush to be a compassionate conservative.*

Politically, Mr Bush may have achieved just what he wanted. He is proving that he is a different kind of con-servative from the zealots who wanted to destroy the De-partment of Education. The bill oozes compassion (the biggest boost in federal spending on poor children in decades), pragmatism (a willingness to boost the size of federal government when it might help) and bipartisan-ship (a new friendship with Ted Kennedy, the chairman of the Senate education committee).

Economist, "Please Sir, Can We Have Some More? George Bush and Educa-tion Reform," December 22, 2001.

Education and the Workforce, produced a bill that was similar to the Senate's, but without the block-grant provisions. The Republican leadership and a handful of rank-and-file conservatives protested. But President Bush weighed in on Boehner and Miller's side, and the House passed the bill on May 23. The Senate passed its version a few weeks later.

Still, little was settled on the accountability front. The Senate's rejiggered formula was widely seen as too complicated for parents to understand, and the House's formula would run into the same reality-check problems that the Senate's had before it was revised. The conference committee charged with resolving differences between the House and Senate versions of the bill began meeting in late July, but the bill languished in committee as the members squabbled over details small and large.

In the meantime, fears over the shrinking surplus were beginning to dominate debate on Capitol Hill. Democrats charged that Bush's tax cut made it impossible to fund education adequately. Interest groups concerned with some of the testing and accountability requirements began circling.

"There weren't a lot of bipartisan feelings," remembers Bush education adviser Sandy Kress. "[Bush] was concerned. ... The momentum clearly had slowed. He was aware of the mood and the difficulties when we came back from the August recess. We were supposed to be farther along."

Then September 11 intervened. When he first heard of the terrorist attacks on the World Trade Center and the Pentagon, Bush was visiting a Florida elementary school to publicly prod Congress to send him a final bill. Perversely enough, the attacks probably helped get the process back on track by ending the political bickering, congressional aides said. The negotiations were kicked up to the conference's top four members: Reps. Miller and Boehner and Sens. Kennedy and Judd Gregg, R-N.H. The thorniest issue—the definition of a failing school—was resolved by the Big Four by late September.

Details

Under the new definition, states must design a plan to raise the children in several demographic groups—black, white, Hispanic, poor, and disabled—to a "proficient" level of achievement on state tests within 12 years. States determine what a proficient score will be and choose an initial goal for the percentage of students in each group that will attain a proficient grade that year. They must raise that bar over time, so that each state reaches 100 percent proficiency 12 years later. If a school does not meet the performance goal for one demographic group, but reduces the number of children who are not proficient by 10 percent, the school will avoid federal penalties. Schools that don't meet either goal will be labeled failing. . . .

The new testing requirement exemplifies Bush's tough-love approach to education reform. "I understand taking tests aren't [sic] fun," the self-proclaimed C student at Yale University told the crowd at Hamilton High. "Too bad." One of the least debated provisions, the requirement for annual testing, is probably the biggest change in the 2002 law. Though the numbers vary depending on how you read the new law, 15 states currently [as of 2002] meet the annual testing requirement in math, 17 in reading, and 24 have established a science test, according to the Education Commission of the States. . . .

The bill Bush signed also requires that the National Assessment of Educational Progress (NAEP) be given in every state every other year in math and reading, but the results cannot influence whether a school is designated as failing. Initially, Bush had proposed that NAEP be administered every year as a national barometer for the state tests. Currently, NAEP is administered in those subjects every four years in about 40 states, a number that fluctuates from test to test depending on which states decline to participate.

The 1994 legislation only suggested penalties for schools that failed to improve student test scores, but Clinton's 1999 proposal, which never made it into law, would have required that states intervene in perpetually failing schools. "The Bush administration took the Clinton administration's ideas and ran with them," said one bemused Democratic congressional aide who worked at the Department of Education under Clinton.

Incremental Successes

The new law sets out a timeline of increasingly severe sanctions to nudge recalcitrant schools along. If a school fails to meet annual state test-score goals for two years, students can transfer to another public school in the district. The failing school also receives extra money to revamp academic programs. After three years of failure, the district must use 5 percent of the money it receives for poor children under the federal Title I program's "Basic Grants" section to pay for outside tutoring services. After four failing years, a school must make significant structural changes, such as revamping the curriculum or firing staff, and may be eligible for a state takeover the following year. At no point does a state or school lose money if it continues producing poor results, although districts eventually have to divert federal money to pay for tutoring services.

Building on the work of one's predecessors can produce success stories. That's just what Bush did as governor of Texas. His reforms expanded those of former governor Ann Richards, whose reforms built on those in places like Dallas and previous statewide efforts led by, of all people, Ross Perot. Dallas, it happens, is where then-school board president Sandy Kress initiated accountability—using standardized tests to reward and sanction schools. "This is our theme," Kress said. "We may not know a lot of music in Texas, but we can sing the song we know well."

The Bush administration tried to set a new tone the night after the president signed the education bill, when Secretary of Education Rod Paige invited 30 state education chiefs to Mount Vernon to discuss the new law and his expectations for the states. After dining on pork and pumpkin mousse, Paige made his pitch: The old days of waivers and delays and closing our eyes to enforcement problems are over. . . .

Sustaining the momentum on enforcement may be the administration's biggest challenge. "Paige is saying he won't give any waivers. Now we shall see. I hope that he can keep the pressure on," says Jack Jennings of the Center on Education Policy. "Elections come up. Is Bush going to deny [New York] Gov. [George] Pataki federal aid when he's running for reelection, if the state has not met its testing requirements?" (Money can be withheld from a state for not complying with the requirements of the law, but not for poor results.)

Even with a troubled economy and continuing worries about terrorism, education remains a high-level concern among voters. Bush's education record will no doubt play an important role in the next election. That means the person who will ultimately be held most accountable in the eyes of the public for reforming the schools is President Bush.

Bush's Education Plan Is Confusing and Self-Defeating

Peter Schrag

Peter Schrag argues in the following viewpoint that Bush's main education policy, the No Child Left Behind Act, fails to accomplish what it was designed to do. Instead of ensuring that all schools provide minimum education standards for children as Bush touted, Schrag contends that the plan has disadvantaged poor and minority children. The law also has confused many parents and school administrators because it has produced a bewildering array of "report cards" and standards. The most significant problem with the policy, according to Schrag, is that it bleeds money from public school systems, which must fund the new programs on existing budget shortfalls. Schrag is an education writer; author of *Paradise Lost: California's Experience, America's Future*; and former editorial page editor of the *Sacramento Bee*.

WELL BEFORE HE BECAME PRESIDENT, GEORGE W. BUSH had made his education plan, the No Child Left Behind Act, the showcase of "compassionate conservatism"—meaning, in the conventional shorthand, a conservative route to liberal ends. Its objective was to force schools to close the huge racial achievement gaps in Amer-

Peter Schrag, "Bush's Education Fraud: The No Child Left Behind Act Is Self-Defeating, Confusing, and Underfunded," *The American Prospect*, vol. 15, February 2004, pp. 28–41. Copyright © 2004 by The American Prospect, Inc. All rights reserved. Reproduced with permission from *The American Prospect*, 5 Broad St., Boston, MA 02109.

ican education, to pay attention to the poor and minority kids they had so often neglected, and to make every child "proficient" in reading and math by the year 2014. The law's name itself was a rip-off of "Leave No Child Behind," the longtime rallying cry of Marian Wright Edelman's Children's Defense Fund. When Bush signed the legislation in January 2002, two liberal Democrats, Massachusetts Sen. Edward Kennedy and California Rep. George Miller, were the co-stars of the White House photo op.

But in the past two years [2002–2004], No Child Left Behind (NCLB)—formally just an extension of the Johnson-era Elementary and Secondary Education Act of 1965, but in practice probably the most sweeping nationalization of school policy in the nation's history—has left a lot behind, including no end of confusion, uncertainty and resentment.

The law itself, the administration's failure to fund it as promised, and the uneven and sometimes incomprehensible way it's been managed by the U.S. Department of Education have begun to generate so many difficulties and so much backlash, particularly among state legislators, that the program could well implode and take down two decades of state educational reforms with it. In the process, it would also end the best hope—all the law's difficulties notwithstanding—that America's poor and minority children have for getting better schools, higher standards and the attention they deserve.

The Plan

The law's basic objectives were simple:

• Create an accountability system of tests, graduation rates, and other indicators that would force individual schools and districts to make adequate yearly progress by raising not only school-wide test scores but the achievement levels of every major subgroup of students—African Americans, Latinos, English language learners, low-income students, special-education students—to a state-defined

tions for NCLB fall $8 billion short of what was authorized by the bill. "We were all suckered into it," said Rep. Dick Gephardt (D-Mo.), who voted for the measure. "It's a fraud."

The underfunding complaints are accompanied by studies indicating that the states' costs of meeting NCLB requirements are running far beyond the money that the federal government is providing. In what's probably the most frequently cited report, published [in 2003] in *Phi Delta Kappan*, William J. Mathis, a Vermont school administrator, concluded that in seven of the 10 states he surveyed, school spending would have to increase 24 percent to comply with all the requirements of NCLB. According to Mathis, Texas, the largest of the states studied, would have to spend $6.9 billion more, roughly doubling the state's school budget. "We're being asked to do more with nothing," said Bob Holmes, who chairs the Georgia House Committee on Education.

Mathis' estimates are controversial: Parsing out real NCLB cost figures is a squishy process. But there's no doubt that at a time of extremely tight state budgets, the law has, said one school superintendent, made everybody crazy. In a survey of principals and superintendents published late in 2003, Public Agenda found that nearly 90 percent regarded NCLB as an unfunded mandate. More than 60 percent said NCLB "will require many adjustments before it can work"; 30 percent said it probably wouldn't work at all. Most significantly, perhaps, the Public Agenda report noted "a noteworthy discrepancy between what NCLB calls for in terms of 'highly qualified' teachers and what superintendents and principals say they need from new teachers." Among those qualifications: the ability to maintain order and discipline in the classroom, to work with students whose background is different from their own and to establish working relationships with parents.

All of that has generated increasing levels of backlash. In at least three states—Minnesota, New Hampshire and

Hawaii—legislators passed or seriously debated resolutions urging those states to withdraw from NCLB even though it means losing the federal money that's tied to it. Otherwise, said a Hawaii Democrat, NCLB is "going to label a lot of excellent schools as failing." In Oregon, Gov. Ted Kulongoski was said to be considering joining up with the National Education Association, the nation's largest teachers' union, in a suit challenging the law as an unfunded mandate.

Testing Is Not Teaching

A retired professor at the University of New Hampshire argues that the focus on Bush's education plan prepares students for tests rather than help them develop as thinkers.

Testing is not teaching. Instead of preparing children for tests, teachers need to be teaching the skills that will, in fact, make them better readers. Teachers should be using this time to give longer assignments to students that require them to read, write, handle different points of view, and solve real problems within the disciplines. . . .

Currently, we are testing what we value, quick thinking. But what about long thinking? Can we discern thinkers like Thomas Jefferson, Albert Einstein, and Charles Darwin, who were self-professed long, slow thinkers? Can we identify and encourage the children who can formulate a question, find the information, structure an evaluation design, and know if they have answered their original question? The problems of a democracy are not solved through single answers but by tough-minded thinkers who sustain thought on one problem for days, months, or years.

Donald H. Graves, "When Testing Lowers Standards," *Reading Today*, vol. 19, April/May 2002, p. 20.

Rigging the System

In most states, however, there's a subtler strategy. Some have lowered their proficiency benchmarks to make their numbers look better. Among them are Michigan, which claimed it really was just making its system more realistic and comparable to other states, and Colorado and Texas, which lowered the passing score on their own tests to reduce the failure rate. Because standards vary so widely, eighth-grade students labeled proficient in Wisconsin are ranked in the 89th percentile in one national survey; a proficient ranking in Montana puts you in the 36th percentile. More pervasive still: Because NCLB says all students must be proficient by 2014, some states have drawn—and the federal government has approved—their expected lines of progress so that the biggest required gains are deferred until further out, when they rise steeply toward what's been described as a balloon payment (and when, presumably, most of today's governors, state superintendents and legislators are gone).

Not surprisingly, NCLB is reinforcing the wave of adequacy lawsuits filed by students, community activists and local districts, demanding that states provide resources adequate to the standards and high-stakes tests they've imposed. If students who fail exit exams are denied diplomas, or if teachers and administrators face sanctions for failing to meet standards, the state presumably has a commensurate legal and moral responsibility to provide the resources to allow them to succeed. A recent adequacy decision in Kansas, which ordered that state to restructure its funding, explicitly cited NCLB; so have new suits filed by school districts and others in Nebraska, Missouri and North Dakota.

A Hollow Promise

More broadly, the nonpartisan National Conference of State Legislatures (NCSL) has been warning that cash-strapped states are being squeezed by their own standards, the NCLB mandates and the threat of further lawsuits. [In 2002], said David Shreve, who tracks No Child Left Behind for the NCSL, the reaction to the bill was "very positive." Then, as now, most state officials supported the testing and accountability principles; some even said NCLB was giving them "a needed kick in the butt," as Shreve put it. But after the political costs of the long and extended battles in many other places to get all constituencies behind the states' own accountability plans—parents, the business community, teachers and administrators—many states, Shreve said, don't want to go through the process of getting their various constituencies to support another accountability system. And while the federal mandates were designed to create a single standard, what they've done is create enough confusion among different accountability measures that it could "cause the public to sour on the whole thing.". . .

Given the lack of plausible political alternatives—the fact that nothing has ever put as much emphasis on the academic success of poor and minority children—it's the only real game in town. If NCLB goes, those who'll be most hurt will, once again, be the children who can least afford it. But NCLB badly needs fixing to provide more flexibility in some areas and more rigorous enforcement in others, especially of the provisions mandating better-qualified teachers for poor children. It needs to provide more help and fewer penalties to low-performing schools. And it desperately needs to be better funded. Otherwise it will be just another in a string of hollow promises.

Bush Pursues Policies That Encourage Development at the Expense of the Environment

Margaret Kriz

Margaret Kriz contends in the following selection that Bush has often elevated economic considerations over environmental concerns. Specifically, the administration has used the courts to open areas that were protected from development to commercial activities. She also asserts that Bush has undermined environmental protections by implementing deep budget cuts that hamper federal environmental agencies such as the Environmental Protection Agency. Finally, Bush has tried to weaken major environmental laws such as the Clean Air Act. According to Kriz, industry leaders, particularly in the energy sector, applaud Bush's environmental decisions because they help the nation meet its energy needs. Kriz is a media fellow at the Hoover Institution and the environmental and energy correspondent for the *National Journal*.

Margaret Kriz, "A Pro-Industry Tilt," *The National Journal*, vol. 36, April 3, 2004, pp. 1,028–34. Copyright © 2004 by the National Journal Group, Inc. All rights reserved. Reproduced by permission.

T HE RED ROCK CANYONS AND SANDSTONE BUTTES OF UTAH are as good a place as any to catch a glimpse of just how fundamentally the Bush administration wants to change federal environmental policies. In Utah, more than 3 million acres, including Moquith Mountain and Parunu- weap Canyon, are designated as wilderness study areas that might one day be added to the nation's permanent inven- tory of wilderness lands.

Environmentalists say the ecologically fragile sites are being overrun by thousands of recreational off-road vehi- cles and argue that, by law, Interior Department regulators are required to protect the study areas until Congress de- cides what to do with them. The environmentalists have sued the Bush administration over the matter, in a case that was heard by the Supreme Court on March 29 [2003].

Bush administration attorneys are asking the nation's top court to reverse a lower-court decision and use *Norton v. Southern Utah Wilderness Alliance* to embrace a narrow interpretation of the disputed land-preservation law. In the administration's view, the public may challenge only final and specific land-management decisions and has no right to sue over the stewardship of lands that are merely being studied for possible protection. The White House in- sists that if the high court allows the Utah lawsuit to go for- ward, environmentalists will flood the courts with land- use challenges.

Shifting the Balance

[George W.] Bush's effort to limit environmental lawsuits is opposed by eight former chairmen of the White House's own Council on Environmental Quality [CEQ], and by 15 state attorneys general who filed a joint friend-of-the- court brief with the Supreme Court siding with the envi- ronmentalists. CEQ chairmen who served under Republi- can Presidents [Richard] Nixon, [Gerald] Ford, and George H.W. Bush are among those who lined up against the current administration's stand.

Since George W. Bush became president, federal regulators have significantly shifted the balance away from preserving federal lands and toward opening them up for more commercial activity. In its highest-profile land battle, the White House continues to push Congress—so far unsuccessfully—to allow oil drilling in Alaska's Arctic National Wildlife Refuge.

This administration's pro-development tilt is no surprise: Bush ran for office promising to expand domestic oil and gas production on federal lands. But despite his determined steps to rewrite environmental and energy policies, the president has not significantly increased U.S. energy production or made the United States less dependent on foreign oil.

As the president's re-election campaign shifts into high gear, Republicans have launched an aggressive effort to counter green groups' contention that Bush is the most anti-environmental president in modern times. The White House is enlisting moderate Republicans to refute charges that Bush and the Republican-controlled Congress have rolled back environmental protections. "If you get rid of the emotion and look at the merits, President Bush has done plenty on the environment," said Robert E. Grady, a venture capitalist in San Francisco who served as an environmental adviser in California Gov. Arnold Schwarzenegger's campaign and as an environmental staffer in George H.W. Bush's White House.

Energy Development

Meanwhile, the current Bush administration is using its national energy strategy, issued in May 2001, as a blueprint to speed up energy development on federal lands and to ease pollution controls on the nation's coal-fired power plants. By contrast, the Clinton administration increased the level of protection on millions of acres of federal land by creating new national monuments and barring road-building on large tracts of the national forests. To combat air pollution, Clinton-era regulators cracked down on coal-fired power plants that had expanded without installing up-to-date pollution-control equipment as required.

Bush officials insist they are adhering to the nation's strict ecological and health-protection standards while working to boost energy development and to lower the cost of complying with pollution-control laws. "It's important to note that in many of these areas we are pushing further than any previous administration" to protect the environment, James L. Connaughton, chairman of Bush's Council on Environmental Quality, said in an interview. "But environmentalists always want to push further."

Interior Secretary Gale Norton, meanwhile, asserts that the Bush administration is safeguarding the nation's crown jewels: its national parks and wilderness lands. "There are many areas that are off-limits and that stay off-limits," she said. "We're not proposing to make any change there. But most of our lands are multiple-use lands, and the directive that we have from Congress is to use those lands for a variety of purposes."

Energy-industry officials praise the Bush administration's efforts to open more federal property to oil and gas development. "This administration has placed a priority on domestic energy production and understands the value it has on the economy and jobs," said Daniel T. Naatz, federal resources director at the Independent Petroleum Association of America. "In the previous administration, that clearly wasn't the case."

But critics counter that the administration is reinterpreting the nation's conservation and environmental laws in ways that benefit Bush's political supporters in industry but harm sensitive ecosystems and overall environmental quality. "What they've done is institute a new policy: making oil and gas development the dominant use of public lands wherever oil and gas resources happen to exist," argued Dave Alberswerth, director of the Wilderness Society's Bureau of Land Management program. "This administration has no land-conservation ethic at all. And they're trying to figure out ways to roll back those protections that have existed."

Phil Clapp, president of the National Environmental Trust, agrees. "The president has proposed delaying cleanup of air pollution and mercury contamination from utilities by a decade," he said. "He is delaying cleanup of toxic-waste sites and is shifting the cost from pollution companies to taxpayers." Clapp summed up his views this way: "On environmental policy, the White House can try to put lipstick on this pig, but the American public still knows it's a pig."

Jeopardizing the Nation's National Parks?

The administration's critics also complain that Bush's deep budget cuts are jeopardizing the management of national parks. But what has the critics most up in arms is the administration's systematic attempt to work under the public's radar to reinterpret and rewrite the little-noticed federal regulations that are the heart and soul of environmental protection. In many cases, the administration has bypassed Congress and used existing regulatory authority to shift the balance toward more oil and gas drilling on federal lands.

For example, in February [2004], the Interior Department began selling oil and gas leases on Utah lands that the Clinton administration had designated as candidates for wilderness protection. The latest move came after Secretary Norton signed an April 2003 agreement with then-Gov. Mike Leavitt of Utah that dropped wilderness study protections on 2.6 million acres. Since then, the Bush administration has allowed energy developers to lease 14 parcels that include acreage—including lands bordering Dinosaur National Monument—that would have been protected under the Clinton decree.

The Norton-Leavitt agreement also included the controversial contention that the Clinton administration had had no legal right to identify new wilderness study areas. "The previous administration tried to create administrative wilderness study areas, but only Congress has the authority to create those," Norton said in an interview. Environmental advocates are challenging both the Utah agreement and Norton's interpretation of the law. They note that Presidents [Ronald] Reagan and George H.W. Bush also designated wilderness study areas.

If Bush wins re-election, administration officials and industry lobbyists suggest, his team will expand its efforts to revise the nation's bedrock environmental laws so that there are fewer obstacles to development, both on public lands and elsewhere.

Along with making regulatory changes, Bush has pushed land-use legislation through Congress. His administration, for example, won congressional approval of legislation aimed at thinning fire-prone forests and allowing increased logging on federal lands—a program the White House dubbed the "Healthy Forests Initiative." But the administration has been less successful at selling Bush's 2002 attempt to rewrite the Clean Air Act, which the White House calls its "Clear Skies Initiative." And a massive energy bill, which includes many of Bush's energy-development proposals, has been bogged down by policy disputes among House and Senate Republicans.

Looking to a second term, the Bush White House hopes to finally succeed with its bids to rewrite the Clean Air Act and to pass energy legislation that focuses on boosting production. Several industry officials also predict that Bush's re-election would pave the way for rewriting the Endangered Species Act, the Clean Water Act, and other environmental-protection statutes, which this administration has already weakened by winning congressional exemptions for all Defense Department lands.

Trouble, Trouble, Trouble

Almost from the beginning of Bush's presidency, opinion polls have recorded public unease with his environmental policies. According to an August 2003 CBS News poll, 55 percent of Americans thought Bush had made little or no progress on improving the environment. And a January CNN/*USA Today*/Gallup poll showed that, by 57 percent to 35 percent, the public considered Democrats better than Republicans at handling environmental issues.

Bush's green ratings have never fully recovered from the environmental controversies he sparked during his first months in office. In March 2001, he backtracked on his campaign promise to regulate emissions of carbon dioxide, which scientists have linked to global warming. That flip-flop triggered a firestorm of criticism from environmental groups, Democrats, and moderate Republicans, as well as from European allies who had viewed the campaign promise as evidence that Bush wanted to help craft an international treaty on climate change. Instead, he withdrew the United States from the United Nations' Kyoto treaty negotiations.

Also in March 2001, administration officials shelved a Clinton-era proposal to sharply reduce the level of arsenic permitted in drinking water. Then-Environmental Protection Agency [EPA] Administrator Christie Whitman proposed controls that were more stringent than the existing arsenic standards, but less strict than the Clinton plan. Hit by a furious backlash, the EPA eventually adopted the Clinton proposal.

Industry's Bidding

Bush's approach to environmental policy came under serious scrutiny again in May 2001, when Vice President [Richard] Cheney released the administration's comprehensive national energy policy, which was developed with plenty of input from industry but very little from public-interest groups. The strategy encourages increased development of fossil fuels and nuclear power but includes few new proposals to advance conservation or alternative sources of power, such as solar energy. The Cheney task force's report triggered lawsuits by public-interest groups seeking access to White House records. Critics predict that the documents will prove what virtually everyone already assumes: Industry played a very large role in crafting the new energy policy.

Then, even though [the September 11, 2001, terrorist attacks] shifted public attention away from environmental issues, the EPA's credibility took another hit when air-quality reports from the cleanup at Ground Zero showed that Whitman had wrongly assured rescue workers and New Yorkers on September 15, 2001, that the air there was safe to breathe. A team of investigators later revealed that Whitman had not had sufficient data to offer assurances about overall air quality near the site.

Over the past two years, the EPA's reputation has also been tarnished by a string of accusations from departing enforcement officials. Three who left have publicly accused the Bush administration of undercutting their ability to rein in polluting companies. And in February, 60 prominent scientists, including 20 Nobel laureates, accused the administration of distorting scientific data to try to strengthen its case for policies involving the environment, health care, medical research, and nuclear weaponry.

Industry lobbyists privately acknowledge that the Bush administration's missteps have created credibility problems that color the public's perception of the president's environmental record. Some middle-of-the-road voters have also been disappointed that, when it comes to energy and the environment, Bush has governed to the right of Reagan. "Bush campaigned as a greater moderate than he has turned out to be, particularly on some of these Western public lands issues," said Paul Portney, president of Resources for the Future, an economics-based environmental think tank.

Some insiders assert that the public and the environmental community shouldn't be surprised that Bush and Cheney, both former oil-industry executives, are more sympathetic than Clinton and his vice president were to the desires of the business community. "The support base of this administration is more business-oriented," said Scott H. Segal, an environmental and energy lobbyist with the law firm of Bracewell & Patterson.

For their part, business officials generally welcome the change. William L. Kovacs, a vice president of the U.S. Chamber of Commerce, says that during the Clinton administration, EPA officials were needlessly hostile to business interests. "Now, the EPA volunteers to come over here and give talks," he said. "It's a completely different world."

But in the new world ushered in by his administration, Bush is vulnerable to nonstop attacks by the nation's top environmental groups, which depict him as anything but a friend of the Earth. In this election year [2004], both the League of Conservation Voters and the Sierra Club, which usually focus their electioneering on helping their favorite congressional candidates, are concentrating their money and door-knocking power on denying Bush a second term.

Changing the Climate

Bush's environmental record has been defined by his most controversial actions. Key examples are his decisions not to regulate carbon dioxide emissions and to withdraw from the Kyoto global-warming treaty aimed at controlling worldwide emissions of such greenhouse gases. Analysts across the political spectrum describe those acts as among Bush's most important environmental decisions, though they disagree on how voters should interpret them.

Environmentalists charge that Bush abdicated his responsibility to lead the world on environmental policy. "The climate-change issue is the single most urgent environmental issue of our generation," said Fred Krupp, president of Environmental Defense, one of the most moderate national environmental groups. "The rest of the industrialized world is moving forward with real [greenhouse-gas] reductions," Krupp said. "But, to date, this administration has taken no constructive actions on addressing climate change."

Energy-industry executives, on the other hand, praise the Bush administration for indefinitely delaying mandatory controls on emissions of carbon dioxide and other gases linked to global warming—restrictions they say would have cost billions of dollars and hurt the U.S. economy. They particularly object to provisions in the Kyoto treaty that require the industrialized nations to curb their greenhouse-gas emissions sooner than developing nations, including China and India, must do so. Connaughton, Bush's CEQ chairman, argues that the administration should get credit for pouring what he describes as a record amount of money into research on climate change and for working with industry to develop voluntary programs to cut greenhouse-gas emissions.

Bush's environmental record has also been defined in large measure by Cheney's 2001 national energy policy report. "Whether or not you agree with the policy proposals, you could argue that the administration deserves credit for raising the profile of a national energy plan," said Portney of Resources for the Future.

The White House energy strategy clearly signaled the administration's intention to push for greater oil and gas development, increased use of coal, and construction of additional nuclear power plants—all policies that the administration has aggressively pursued. The Cheney report also called for increased use of renewable energy sources and development of energy-efficient technologies, although the administration has put much less effort into those proposals than into the fossil fuel and nuclear programs.

Shortly after its energy strategy was released, the White House issued an executive order directing regulators to study whether government efforts to preserve federal lands hamper energy development. That order was a low-profile attempt to undermine the Magna Carta of environmental law, the National Environmental Policy Act [NEPA]. That 34-year-old act requires companies to consider the environmental impact of proposed projects that involve federal lands or federal funding.

Companies that bristle at NEPA's requirements applaud Bush's new approach. "The administration is trying to balance these different considerations, with an understanding that energy is vital for the economy," said Barry Russell, president of the Independent Petroleum Association. But environmental critics assert that the White House directive is further evidence that the administration favors commercial development over land preservation. "The policy is way out of whack. Everything's on the auction block," said Mike Matz, executive director of the Campaign for America's Wilderness.

The administration has also found itself in the hot seat over its rejection of Clinton-era rules that required power plants, refineries, and other industrial facilities to install expensive new pollution-control equipment when expanding. Bush's EPA wants to give companies more leeway to grow without having to curb the pollution they emit. But in December, a federal appeals court slapped down Bush's plan, after 12 Northeastern states and several major cities argued that the new rules would subject them to dirtier air.

The Clean Air Act

The White House ranks its planned rewrite of the Clean Act as one of Bush's top environmental initiatives. But that legislation, too, has generated heated controversy. The measure would set up a so-called cap-and-trade program, under which power plants would have to lower their emissions of sulfur dioxide, nitrogen oxides, and mercury by 70 percent beginning in 2018—or buy "credits" from other plants that have cut their emissions below required levels. (A Clinton-era plan would have required that mercury emissions be controlled beginning in 2007.) The Bush administration measure is modeled after the 1990 Clean Air Act amendments—developed under the first President Bush—which created an emissions-trading program that has dramatically lowered power-plant emissions of sulfur dioxide, which causes acid rain.

But unlike the 1990 amendments, this White House's air-pollution legislation would eliminate or postpone the deadlines on several key parts of the Clean Air Act. In the process, critics contend, the administration's bill would cripple efforts to curb air pollution in some regions.

"This administration is cutting all the regulatory backstops out of the law, and substituting the flexible emission-trading program," said Angela Ledlord, director of Clear the Air, an environmental-education group. "That could have serious impacts on the environment."

Power-industry officials, not surprisingly, favor Bush's proposal and his efforts to erase major provisions of the Clean Air Act. "Those regulations are duplicative. They offered no clarity to industry," argued David Owens, executive vice president for business operations at the Edison Electric Institute, an industry group.

Despite the fanfare with which the White House unveiled its Clear Skies Initiative, Bush's proposal has gotten a lukewarm reception on Capitol Hill and is not expected to pass this year. So EPA Administrator Leavitt is focused on trying to use existing regulatory authority to implement the president's cap-and-trade legislation.

Environmentalists and health care groups reserve some of their strongest fire for Bush's proposal to allow power plants to buy and sell credits for emissions of mercury, which can cause brain damage in fetuses and young children. They note that the emissions-trading program would allow the heaviest polluters to buy their way out of having to install new pollution-control equipment. The result might leave some regions with severe mercury-pollution problems.

According to the EPA's own analysis, 630,000 children born each year are at risk for mercury-related developmental problems. The Centers for Disease Control and Prevention estimated that one of every 12 women of child-bearing age has enough mercury in her bloodstream to threaten fetal health. Fears about the health hazards associated with this pollutant led environmental groups, Democrats, and even moderate Republicans to attack the administration's mercury rule, and Leavitt now says he will reassess his agency's approach.

Healthy Forests?

On another environmental battlefield, the White House continues to tout its program to thin the national forests that are most prone to massive fires. Begun as a regulatory program, the administration's forest plan was adopted by Congress in 2003 after wildfires destroyed 2.2 million acres of forestland in the West. The Bush administration says the plan is aimed at clearing underbrush and reducing the number of trees clogging the federal forests as a result of 100 years of aggressive firefighting. Experts say the overgrown forests have combined with years of drought to turn much of the West into a tinderbox. Under Bush's initiative, the government eventually hopes to thin 80 million to 90 million acres of forestlands, according to Mark Rey, undersecretary of Agriculture for natural resources and environment.

Environmental groups object to the parts of the initiative that allow timber companies to remove and sell large, healthy trees to help fund the thinning project. Michael Francis, a forest expert at the Wilderness Society, worries that the logging provisions could be broadly interpreted to allow massive timber cuts. He and other environmental advocates want the Bush administration to focus on thinning the 11 million acres of national forest that are adjacent to homes and towns. Rey said that two-thirds of the program's budget will be targeted to those areas.

Nevertheless, environmentalists accuse the Bush administration of using "Healthy Forests" funds to allow timber companies to cut and sell huge numbers of trees in California's Giant Sequoia National Monument and elsewhere. Rey argues that the sequoia forests need to be aggressively thinned because of the risk of conflagration. "If you want to be able to protect the sequoias, you're going to have to clear the vegetation around these groves," Rey said in an interview. "If you don't, and a fire burns through there, you risk losing the giants."

Despite the environmentalists' worries about Bush's forestry plan, Congress is unlikely to challenge the program if wildfires once again scorch the West this summer. Rey noted that drought conditions continue to plague the Southwest, and experts predict that the 2004 fire season will start early there.

Hook and Bullet

Interior Secretary Norton is a big fan of her department's program to protect the endangered piping plover, a small white-and-sandy-colored bird that nests along beaches. When Norton is peppered with questions about contentious governmental land-use issues, she's been known to remind reporters about the Bush administration's campaign to protect piping plover nesting areas on New York's Long Island. The administration has spent $9.4 million on private stewardship grant programs aimed at encouraging property owners, communities, and conservation groups to voluntarily preserve habitats for declining species like the piping plover.

Norton and others who oversee the administration's

environmental programs say that Bush is not getting proper credit for species-protection advances and other environmental success stories happening on his watch. These officials' complaints are reminiscent of the laments by Bill Reilly, the EPA administrator under Bush I, that the president was never praised for championing legislation to reduce acid rain, restricting oil and gas drilling off U.S. coasts, and supporting international negotiations on global warming.

Republicans argue that environmental activists are more critical of GOP officeholders than of Democratic ones. "There's an open question as to whether a Republican administration can ever go as far as the environmental community would like," Washington lobbyist Segal said.

To change the tenor of the debate over its environmental record, the Bush administration is working with conservation groups that represent hunters and fishers—sometimes known as the "hook-and-bullet" crowd. James D. Range, chairman of the Theodore Roosevelt Conservation Partnership, an alliance of hunting and fishing groups, praised Bush for responding to his members' campaign to preserve wetlands and protect the species that live there. In December, after meeting with Range and other leaders of conservation groups, Bush dropped plans to remove millions of acres from the government's wetlands-protection program.

Range, who served on the staff of then-Sen. Howard Baker, R-Tenn., says of the Bush meeting, "We felt comfortable that we had an ear at the administration listening to us."

Charles Gauvin, president of Trout Unlimited, acknowledged that the Bush administration is playing his group off against national environmental organizations that lean further to the left. "There is a good-cop, bad-cop thing going on in the administration now," he said. "They're saying, 'We'll listen to the hook-and-bullet groups because they're not negative—but the green groups are.'" Nonetheless, Gauvin welcomes the access: "I'm glad they're listening to somebody other than just power-company executives."

If pressed, even most environmental leaders say Bush's record does have some bright spots. They praise EPA's plans to curb air pollution emitted by construction, mining, farming, and other industrial equipment. They also give the White House credit for staying the course on some Clinton pollution-control efforts. For example, Bush regulators have pushed forward with plans to restrict the sulfur allowed in diesel fuel and to impose strict pollution-control requirements on buses and large trucks.

The environmentalists also support the EPA's plans to fight dust and smog—technically known as particulate matter and ozone. And some have been receptive to Leavitt's proposal to create a cap-and-trade program to control emissions of sulfur dioxide and nitrogen oxide from power plants in 29 Eastern states and the District of Columbia. Although environmentalist activists tend to oppose the cap-and-trade approach for mercury emissions, some think that such a program makes sense for sulfur dioxide and nitrogen oxide emissions, which are regional health hazards, not local threats like mercury.

Bush's Energy Policies Favor the Energy Industry

Charles Lewis

The cornerstone of Bush's energy policies is a controversial proposal allowing oil drilling in the Arctic National Wildlife Refuge (ANWR). In the following selection, Charles Lewis examines the controversies surrounding Bush's energy policies, including the actions of his energy task force, led by Vice President Dick Cheney. The author argues that the advisory group crafted policies that favored the large oil companies that had contributed heavily to Bush's presidential campaign. Lewis is the founder and a board member of the Center for Public Integrity, a nonpartisan political research group.

A S THE U.S. SENATE PREPARED TO ADJOURN ON MARCH 19, 2003, partisan politics gave way to a sober acknowledgment that the nation was most likely on the brink of another war. Two days earlier, in a televised address to the nation, George W. Bush issued a stern ultimatum to Iraqi president Saddam Hussein and his sons: leave their country within 48 hours or the U.S. would commence military action there at a time of its choosing. With the clock having technically run out just an hour earlier, Nevada senator Harry Reid, the assistant Democratic leader, took to the floor and somberly closed out the day's business on a bi-partisan note. "As we retire tonight," Reid said, "I think I speak for the entire Senate when I say our thoughts and prayers are with those who have to make this momentous decision, especially the president."

The Arctic National Wildlife Refuge

Earlier that afternoon there was far less unanimity among what's familiarly known as the world's greatest deliberative body, as routine parliamentary arm-twisting turned into a full-scale verbal scuffle. At issue was an amendment de-signed to squash a key component of the president's ener-gy plan: drilling in the Arctic National Wildlife Refuge (known as ANWR), the magnificent home to dozens of species of birds and 45 species of marine and land mam-mals, including wolves, caribou, muskoxen, and polar bears. The previous year, the White House had come up short in its bid to convince lawmakers to authorize drilling in a remote area of the 19-million-acre refuge; this time around, fearing a repeat, administration lobbyists were out in force. The heaviest pro-drilling muscle, however, was provided by Alaska Republican Ted Stevens, whose behav-ior preceding the vote hardly typified the gentlemanly de-meanor for which the U.S. Senate is so well known: "I make this commitment," Stevens said. "People who vote against this today are voting against me, and I will not forget it."

Legislative bluster notwithstanding, opponents of the administration's plan—both in and out of Congress—took issue with more than just the idea of encroaching on this pristine land, whose actual oil reserves have remained an ongoing source of speculation and debate. The previous day, for example, a *Washington Post* editorial had castigat-ed the Bush administration and its congressional allies for including the Arctic-drilling provision in a budget bill rather than letting it run its normal legislative course—that is, debating its merits in committees concerned with the environment. "It is inexcusable for powerful members of Congress to continue to shove legislation affecting Alaska wildlife into unrelated bills simply because it would be impossible to get enough votes any other way," the *Post* proclaimed. Senator John Kerry, who two years earlier had threatened to filibuster any legislation opening "America's Serengeti" to drilling, echoed that view during floor debate. The Massachusetts Democrat, who had formally declared his own presidential aspirations three and a half months earlier, not only objected to the potential for wilderness destruction, but he had another complaint: the oil-drilling provision, he said, had been "slipped into the budget for the specific purpose of trying to bypass the normal rules of the Senate."

This legislative gambit may have angered drilling opponents, but the Bush administration was determined to eke out a victory any way it could get one. Its sights, after all, had been on ANWR and its incalculable energy treasures since the nascent days of this presidency—a position that George W. Bush had unflinchingly articulated during the 2000 campaign. "It will produce a million barrels a day," he argued during a debate with Democratic rival Al Gore. "Today we import a million barrels from Saddam Hussein."

The Task Force

Bush's arrival at the White House, it turned out, had coincided with the California power crisis, which sent electricity rates soaring, pushed the state's two largest utilities to the verge of bankruptcy, shuttered businesses, and, thanks to rolling blackouts, left angry consumers in the dark—hard times, the new administration warned, that might be relived elsewhere without the imposition of nationwide energy reforms. But the California situation notwithstanding, Bush had already placed this issue near the top of his domestic agenda. In fact, just nine days after taking office, he established a task force—with Vice President Dick Cheney at the helm—charged with devising the administration's energy policies. The National Energy Policy Development Group counted among its members the secretaries of energy, interior, and transportation. Its mission was to "develop a national energy policy designed to help the private sector, and as necessary and appropriate federal, state, and local governments, promote dependable, affordable, and environmentally sound production and distribution of energy."

Skeptics had no doubt that whatever emerged from the months-long exercise would include recommendations to extract ANWR's subterranean riches. But some, like the *New York Times*, also aimed their barbs elsewhere: "It hardly signals a balanced approach to put Vice President Dick Cheney, also an oil man, in charge of a task force aimed at developing an energy strategy to reduce America's 'reliance on foreign oil' and 'bring more energy into the marketplace,'" the paper said in an editorial.

When the task force report was finally made public, on May 17, 2001, it highlighted a host of recommendations urging the increased use of renewable and alternative energy, from wind and solar power to hydrogen fuel cells. If conservationists weren't exactly jubilant, however, it was because of the report's other recommendations, which, to no one's surprise, included exploring ANWR for oil.

This was welcome news for BP, ChevronTexaco, and ExxonMobil, which eagerly sought the rights to drill there. All three, it turns out, have been generous benefactors of George W. Bush's political career. ExxonMobil contributed $117,075 to his campaigns, while BP has given him $96,093 and ChevronTexaco has contributed $82,350, according to figures compiled by the Center for Public Integrity. And the trio share another distinction: each donated $100,000 to the Bush-Cheney inaugural, BP via the corporation and the oil giant's two peers via top company officials.

The task force report also held the promise of lucrative prizes for other oil and gas firms, including more development offshore and on public lands. Records compiled by the Center show that Bush's list of career patrons includes energy industry stalwarts Shell Oil Company ($82,412), El Paso Corporation ($68,634), Phillips Petroleum Company ($55,861), and Occidental Petroleum Corporation ($38,179); also included on the roster are such lower-profile—yet nonetheless generous—players as Hunt Oil Company ($152,250), Alkek Oil Corporation ($126,000), and Koch Industries ($79,950), whose core businesses include petroleum and natural gas. Top officials of El Paso, Hunt, and Shell, records show, were members of the Governor's Business Council [GBC], the group of industry bigwigs who advised Bush during his tenure as Texas's chief executive. At the time, the GBC's elite ranks also included the president of Halliburton Company, Richard B. Cheney.

The administration's energy blueprint was similarly kind to the electric utility industry: recommendations included legislation that would repeal the Public Utility Holding Company Act, which bars the use of profits from regulated utility businesses to fund unrelated enterprises, and reform the Public Utility Regulatory Policies Act of 1978, which was designed, in part, to both augment electric utility generation with more efficiently produced power and ensure fair rates for consumers. The industry's push to reform these laws boasted some notable lobbying clout with the new administration; the presidents of the Edison Electric Institute and FirstEnergy Corporation were among George W. Bush's fundraising Pioneers. So was Erle Nye, the chairman and chief executive of TXU Corporation (formerly known as Texas Utilities), who was also a member of the Governor's Business Council during Bush's tenure. Edison, FirstEnergy, and TXU have all given thousands to Bush's campaigns (the latter ranks thirty-sixth on the list of career patrons, with contributions of $159,299, according to calculations by the Center). What's more, Anthony J. Alexander, the president and chair of

FirstEnergy, and Erle Nye, of TXU Energy, contributed $100,000 to the Bush-Cheney inaugural. And if Nye's clout wasn't quite sufficient, his company's lobbying roster included Diane Allbaugh, whose husband, Joe Allbaugh, was Bush's campaign manager during the 2000 election.

The Energy Sector Cheers

Across the board, in fact, energy producers found reason to cheer the recommendations of Dick Cheney's task force. The coal industry, for example, which in recent years has been something of an energy-sector pariah, received a wholehearted endorsement from the task force report: "If rising U.S. electricity demand is to be met," the document noted, "then coal must play a significant role." To that end, the task force suggested that the Department of Energy invest $2 billion over 10 years to fund research in clean coal technologies, and that current research-and-development tax credits be made permanent. Among those who stand to benefit from the migration back to coal is James "Buck" Harless, a West Virginia coal and timber baron who served as a Bush Pioneer, and who later donated $100,000 to the presidential inaugural. Harless, one of more than thirty energy industry officials who served on the Bush Transition Energy Advisory Team (Erle Nye, of TXU, served as well), seems to have maintained his connections within the White House: according to the *Charleston Gazette*, Harless was apparently behind the appointment of Michael Castle to a position created specially for him in the Philadelphia office of the Environmental Protection Agency—the regional office whose territory includes West Virginia. Castle, formerly West Virginia's top environmental official, worked as a consultant to the coal industry following his departure from state government. He has also been an engineer and once even ran his own small coal company.

The nuclear energy industry, which for years lived under a cloud spewed by [the near reactor meltdown at]

Three Mile Island, saw would-be allies in Bush and Cheney, and as such gave them more than a quarter of a million dollars during the 2000 campaign. It was money well spent: the task force report included a recommendation that the President "support the expansion of nuclear energy in the United States as a major component of our national energy policy." And much to the industry's relief, the report also urged extension of the Price-Anderson Act, which both limits the amount of insurance that nuclear operators must carry and caps their liability in case of catastrophic accident.

But the industry's greatest favor came in the form of administration support for a legislative end-game to a twenty-year battle for an unlikely prize: Yucca Mountain, located in a desolate, federally protected tract of desert about 100 miles northwest of Las Vegas. While the industry has long considered Yucca Mountain a suitable place to store its radioactive spent nuclear fuel—the Energy Department first explored the idea in 1978—Nevada legislators joined environmentalists in condemning the notion, citing potential health and safety risks. And legislators elsewhere later joined the opponents, their fears stoked by the possibility that cross-country nuclear waste shipments, whether by train or truck, would make alluring targets for terrorists. Prior to a vote on the matter, then Senate majority leader Thomas Daschle, Democrat of South Dakota, voiced another concern: "We are being forced to decide this issue prematurely, without sufficient scientific information, because this administration is doing the bidding of special interests that simply want to make the deadly waste they have generated someone else's problem," he said.

The nuclear power industry tied its very survival to congressional approval of this plan: with storage space for spent nuclear fuel dwindling, lobbyists and industry officials argued, some utilities faced the prospect of soon shuttering their reactors. To ensure that the industry got its

way, President Bush played a deft game of political hard-
ball. Utah's senators, for instance, were given an ultimatum; if the storage facility isn't built in Nevada, it would be
relocated to their home state.

In the end, Bush and Cheney—and the industry that
supported them—got their way, but the plan still has to
survive court challenges. Although the president has used
bill-signing ceremonies to tout his environmental credentials, no reporters were permitted to witness the signing of
this legislation, on July 23, 2002. But a top industry spokes-
man was not so low-key: "This is a great day for U.S. energy security and commonsense environmentalism," Joe
Colvin, president and CEO of the Nuclear Energy Institute, the industry's lobbying arm, proclaimed. Among
Colvin's other credentials: a place on the Bush administration's Transition Energy Advisory Team.

Legal Fisticuffs

While Dick Cheney's national energy policy task force report received considerable scrutiny, many of its conclu-
sions proved to be less controversial than the process by
which the document was created—a closed-door series of
off-the-record meetings whose participant roster was
guarded like a list of Skull & Bones Society recruits. In fact,
the administration's insistence that details of task force
meetings were unfit for public—even congressional—con-
sumption provoked an unprecedented legal melee that, for
some historians, politicians, and legal scholars, ended with
what they deemed the subversion of open government.

The battle was first joined on April 19, 2001, when two
veteran Democratic U.S. representatives—John Dingell of
Michigan and Henry Waxman of California—asked the
General Accounting Office [GAO] to immediately under-
take an investigation of the energy task force, which, they
noted, had been meeting for at least a month. Underlying
their request, the lawmakers wrote, were apparent efforts

to shield the task force's membership and deliberations from public scrutiny.

"The process of energy policy development needs sunshine," the duo added in their letter to David Walker, who as comptroller general of the United States heads the GAO. "At a minimum, the public has the right to know who serves on this task force; what information is being presented to the task force and by whom it is being given; and to learn of the costs involved in the gathering of the facts."

Concurrent with their request to the GAO, which serves as the audit and investigative arm of Congress, Dingell and Waxman presented Andrew Lundquist, the executive director of the task force, with a series of detailed questions about the group's operation. Of particular concern, they wrote, was the decision to meet behind closed doors and exclude "certain parties" from participation in discussions—a possible violation, they contended, of the Federal Advisory Committee Act [FACA], which mandates openness and public participation for those boards, commissions, and similar entities that advise the executive branch of the federal government. Three days earlier, in an article about the task force's penchant for secrecy, the *Washington Post* had publicly identified those excluded parties: "Environmental groups complain that Cheney won't meet with their leaders," the paper reported, "while the vice president sits down with a parade of industry officials."

On May 10, the GAO informed Dingell and Waxman that it had deemed their request to be within its scope of authority and would therefore proceed with a study of the energy task force. But the congressmen already knew that GAO investigators would no doubt face imposing hurdles. A week earlier, the counsel to Vice President Cheney had informed the two House members that, to his way of thinking, FACA did not apply to the energy task force. As a result, attorney David Addington labeled their request legally specious and rebuffed their demands for information, thereby laying the groundwork for a challenge that might presumably cast Cheney as an overly secretive obstructionist.

But if the White House was at all concerned about the legal jousting, it wasn't apparent. Following a two-week campaign to engender support for his energy policies, Bush released the task force report and set about to convince both the public and wary party loyalists of its virtues. He faced a formidable task: a CNN/*USA Today*/Gallup poll revealed only a tepid response to the energy blueprint, with the nation more or less evenly split over its potential merits. What's more, the advantage of Dick Cheney's tie-breaking vote in the 50–50 Senate was suddenly erased by the defection of Vermont Republican James Jeffords, who abandoned his party and became an independent. Among the reasons Jeffords cited for firing his political torpedo: disagreements with the president's positions on energy policy and the environment.

The Task Force Study

As the pundits debated whether Jeffords had left the GOP's hopes of wide-ranging energy reform DOA, the General Accounting Office pressed ahead on its task force study. On June 1, 2001, Comptroller General Walker asked task force attorney David Addington to provide details about the group's meetings, including the names and titles of attendees. Addington refused. Walker asked again three weeks later, but the vice president's counsel only demurred. On July 18, Walker wrote Cheney directly to demand "full and complete access" to the pertinent records, as mandated by the U.S. Code. On August 2, Cheney in turn dispatched memos to the Senate and House of Representatives claiming that Walker's requests exceeded his lawful authority, and that acquiescing to them would "unconstitutionally interfere with the functioning of the Executive Branch."

Cheney never wavered from this position, entrenching

himself in a high-profile bout of legal fisticuffs that would drag on for another 18 months. But if he remained convinced of his statutory footing, his resoluteness was undermined by a growing public perception that withholding the list of task force participants was tantamount to an admission of wrongdoing. "Two reasons may help explain why Cheney is stonewalling," the Los Angeles Times said in an editorial that typified the criticism. "The first is that the administration wants to run future, controversial policies through the vice president's office to shield them from scrutiny and accountability, and it is trying to use this as a model. The other reason is that handing over the list would probably confirm what an embarrassment President Bush's energy plan is."

There was another reason: the CNN/USA Today/Gallup poll that revealed indifference about the president's new energy plan also found that 61 percent of respondents believed energy companies had too much influence over the administration's energy policies. By contrast, only 32 percent of those asked said the energy companies did not wield too much sway. As the Los Angeles Times went on to say in its editorial: "Cheney can't be thrilled about letting Americans see the depth of influence that the oil and gas industry has on the energy plan and in the White House."

A Legal Challenge

While Bush and Cheney fought mightily to squelch all details of the task force meetings, a window into its operations was later provided courtesy of a federal judge. In response to a lawsuit by the Natural Resources Defense Council [NRDC] and Judicial Watch, a nonprofit government watchdog that had previously harangued President Bill Clinton over such matters as his "eleventh-hour pardons," the Department of Energy was ordered to produce thousands of pages of documents that, in some cases, proved to be particularly illuminating. Although heavily edited by the government, with pages missing and large blocks of text deleted, the e-mails, phone logs, and other paperwork nevertheless showed, for example, that over the course of its operation, which stretched from January 2001 to September 2001, the energy task force solicited the views of industry officials and lobbyists while all but ignoring the input of public interest organizations and consumer groups. According to an analysis released in May 2002, the NRDC concluded that industry representatives had 714 direct contacts with task force members while nonindustry representatives had only 29. Another 105 direct contacts could not be definitively categorized, the NRDC reported.

From mid-February to late-July [2001], for instance, Secretary of Energy Spencer Abraham attended 11 task force meetings, one of which was called to release the group's long-awaited report, "Reliable, Affordable, and Environmentally Sound Energy for America's Future." The secretary's calendar entries include:

- February 14, 2001: meeting with the president and two other top officials of the National Association of Manufacturers (which has favored drilling in ANWR and has opposed the Kyoto Protocol global-warming treaty)
- March 14: meeting with oil and gas industry officials, including the chairman and president of the Independent Petroleum Association of America
- March 28: meeting with municipal and public power authorities
- April 3: meeting with the CEO of UtiliCorp United (a Missouri-based distributor of electricity and natural gas, since renamed Aquila, Inc., that is one of 37 companies later accused by the Federal Energy Regulatory Commission of manipulating western U.S. markets during the California energy crisis of 2000–2001)
- April 3: meeting with two officials of the American Coal Company

- April 25: meeting with coal producers at the White House

None of Abraham's meetings, documents show, included representatives of environmental or consumer groups.

Returning Favors?

And there were two other threads that wound their way across the lists of coal, electricity, natural gas, and nuclear power executives and lobbyists who attended task force meetings: many had contributed mightily to Bush and the Republican Party, and their points of view were sometimes included—almost verbatim—in the final energy blueprint. Language in the final report, for instance, was altered from previous drafts to favor Halliburton, Cheney's former employer.

There was also the matter of Enron, George W. Bush's number one career patron, according to a Center for Public Integrity analysis. In January 2002, a month after the once high-flying energy firm had filed for bankruptcy, the White House told Henry Waxman that Cheney or his aides had met with officials of the company six times during the previous year. One such meeting, which lasted a half-hour, involved the vice president and Kenneth Lay, Enron's chairman. Following the meeting, the White House added a provision to the final energy report potentially favorable to Enron.

On January 30, 2002, the General Accounting Office announced that it would soon proceed with its lawsuit against Cheney—a planned action it had shelved following the terrorist attacks of the previous September 11 [2001]. In a letter to the White House and congressional leaders, Comptroller General Walker was at the same time both resolute and rueful about his decision: "In our view, failure to pursue this matter could lead to a pattern of records access denials that would significantly undercut GAO's ability to assist Congress in exercising its legislative and oversight authorities. . . . This will be the first time that GAO has filed suit to enforce our access rights against a federal official," he wrote. "We hope it is the last time that we will have to do so."

In the end, this maiden attempt proved fruitless. On December 9, 2002, U.S. District Judge John D. Bates, a George W. Bush appointee, ruled that the GAO has no legal standing to sue the vice president. Two months later, the GAO—its annual budget dependent on the Republican-controlled Congress—grudgingly decided against appealing the ruling, thereby granting the White House the wish to which it had so steadfastly and adamantly clung: to forever keep secret the details of Cheney's private meetings with industry. (Judicial Watch and the Sierra Club sued to make public certain task force details, and their lawsuit, which in July 2003 survived a key federal appeals court challenge, may ultimately reveal those documents the GAO had sought.)

With all eyes on Iraq, however, Judge Bates's noteworthy decision received little attention. In fact, as the buildup to the invasion proceeded, otherwise controversial proposals like drilling in ANWR went forth without the usual scrutiny of the press and public. But if Bush and Cheney hoped to quietly win approval for this coveted piece of their energy scheme, they were to be disappointed: on March 19, 2003, by a margin of 52 to 48, the Senate voted to prevent consideration of drilling in the Alaskan wildlife refuge. The fight was over—for now. As Alaskan Republican senator Ted Stevens warned: "It's never decided until we win."

If Bush and Cheney have their way, they'll have another chance to record that victory. In early March [2003], while an increasing number of U.S. troops prepared for an assault on Iraq, and while a fractured nation debated the wisdom and efficacy of the intended military action, the president authorized his advisors to quietly begin planning his reelection strategy. Details of the embryonic effort were characteristically hard to come by, although strategists did let on that the game plan called for raising some $200 million (twice what he raised during the 2000 elections), and perhaps as much as $250 million. By mid-April, when the conventional warfare in Iraq had more or less ended, sources made it known that, a month hence, Bush would resume his political fundraising activities at a $2,500-a-plate "President's Dinner," cosponsored by the Republican House and Senate campaign committees. And in May, as Bush prepared for his return to the campaign trail, his aides unveiled yet another fundraising wrinkle: those raising $100,000 would again earn the coveted Pioneer title, but only those raising $200,000 would be included in the new, more elite club known as the Rangers. Soliciting so much money may have seemed like an overly ambitious goal, but by early July, just six weeks after Bush's first campaign outing, the Rangers roster already included at least a half-dozen names. And there was apparently a large contingent on their way to joining those fundraising virtuosos: during those same six weeks, the Bush-Cheney reelection committee registered more than $34 million in donations, more than all nine announced Democratic challengers combined.

CHAPTER

5

ASSESSING BUSH'S TRANSITION AND POLITICAL STRATEGY

The Bush Team Managed an Impressive Transition

Joseph A. Pika, John Anthony Maltese,
and Norman C. Thomas

The closeness of the 2000 presidential election, in which Bush
won with 271 electoral votes while his opponent Al Gore received 267 electoral votes (but received 540,000 more popular
votes than did Bush), caused delays in the transition to the new
Bush administration. It was not until January 6, 2001, that Bush
was officially declared the winner. Nonetheless, Joseph A. Pika,
John Anthony Maltese, and Norman C. Thomas argue in the
following selection that Bush managed one of the better presidential transitions. They note that Bush's transition team efficiently managed the problems caused by the delay (including
the assembling of the Cabinet). The success of the team was
mainly due to the experience of its members, including Vice
President Dick Cheney. Pika is on the faculty of the University
of Delaware, Maltese teaches at Johns Hopkins University, and
Thomas is a distinguished professor who retired from the University of Cincinnati.

T HE CIRCUMSTANCES SURROUNDING THE CONTESTED 2000
presidential election did not make the new president's
transition to power an easy task. Uncertainty about who

Joseph A. Pika, John Anthony Maltese, and Norman C. Thomas, *The Politics of the
Presidency*. Washington, DC: CQ Press, 2002. Copyright © 2002 by the Congressional
Quarterly, Inc. All rights reserved. Reproduced by permission.

had won dogged both candidates from the early evening of election day (November 7). The television networks first declared Al Gore the winner at 7:48 P.M. EST—even before all polls were closed—based on exit surveys of voters leaving election precincts. By 10:00 P.M. the networks were forced to retract their declaration and announce instead that the election was too close to call. In the early morning hours of November 8, George W. Bush gained momentum. Shortly after 2:00 A.M. the networks began calling the election again—this time for Bush. Prompted by the networks' projections, Gore telephoned Bush to concede around 2:40 A.M., but almost immediately it appeared that the networks had erred again by prematurely calling the outcome. New returns showed that the election was still in doubt, and by 3:00 A.M. the networks had declared the race too close to call. The new returns, coupled with the realization that Florida law required an automatic machine recount when the election margin was so close, led Gore to telephone Bush a second time, shortly after 3:15 A.M., to withdraw his concession. Those confounding hours paved the way for weeks of uncertainty about which of the two candidates would actually take office. . . .

Challenging, Abbreviated Transition

A normal transition to power proved impossible in the wake of the 2000 presidential contest because there was no clear winner until weeks after election day. The federal government provides funds and office space for presidents-elect to mount their transitions. In 2000 the government allocated $5.3 million in transition funds. It also provided a two-story, ninety-thousand-square-foot office building in Washington, D.C., one capable of holding 540 people and equipped with three hundred computers and phones. The building even had its own zip code: 20270. The General Accounting Office, however, refused to release the money or open the office space to either of the candidates until the outcome of the election had been resolved. This refusal was a problem for both candidates. After all, the transition period is an essential and—even under the best of circumstances—*small* window of opportunity to establish a new White House team and prepare an agenda for the critical first hundred days of the new administration.

James P. Pfiffner has emphasized that presidents must "hit the ground running" after they take the oath of office. As Pfiffner explains, presidents "want to take advantage of the 'mandate' from the voters and create a 'honeymoon' with Congress." Early victories in implementing their policy goals "may provide the 'momentum' for further gains. This desire to move fast is driven by the awareness that power is fleeting." Likewise, Paul Light has argued that a president's "political capital" decreases over time. As political capital is expended, a president's influence and ability to accomplish his goals is diminished. That is why presidents are so eager to move quickly to implement their policy goals. Their eagerness to accomplish their goals, though, comes at a time when they and their staffs are new to their jobs and relatively inexperienced. Thus, Pfiffner notes that a president's "greatest opportunity to work his will comes when he has the least ability to do it effectively; this is what makes planning an effective transition so critical." Quite simply the ability to move quickly and effectively depends on a well-organized transition that gets key players in position in a timely way and sets the stage for early policy planning.

Without knowing the outcome of the election, and without federal funds and office space to help them, both candidates were hampered in their transition planning. A concern for public relations also limited the extent to which either Bush or Gore could proceed—at least publicly—with transition planning in the days immediately after the election. Choosing a cabinet and making other transition plans before being declared the winner could look presumptuous, even unseemly, but failing to do so could handicap the new administration. The task was particularly daunting for the Republicans because they had been out of power for eight years and had an estimated three thousand positions to fill.

Taking the Reins of Government

On November 27, three weeks after election day, Dick Cheney—Bush's running mate and transition head—held a news conference to announce that the Bush team would open a privately funded transition headquarters in McLean, Virginia. As a result of Harris's certification of Bush as the winner of the Florida election, Bush had declared himself "president-elect." Although court rulings were still pending, Cheney chastised the Democrats for not conceding. "Vice President Gore and Senator Lieberman are apparently still unwilling to accept the outcome," he told reporters. "That is unfortunate in light of the penalty that may have to be paid at some future date if the next administration is not allowed to prepare to take the reins of government.". . .

Considering the circumstances, the Bush transition went smoothly—more smoothly, in fact, than Bill Clinton's, which got off to a remarkably slow start after the 1992 election. Clinton took six weeks to make *any* appointments, and it took a full ten months after he was sworn in for all of his appointees to be confirmed by the Senate. Taking a different approach, Bush seemed to have his major appointments lined up within four weeks of election day, although he held back any cabinet announcements until December 16—three days after Gore conceded and just under six weeks after the election.

If Clinton's transition stood out for its problems. Bush's did so for its discipline in the face of major obstacles. Part of the problem for the Clinton transition team came from the inexperience of Clinton and his aides, most of whom had never before served in government. In contrast, Bush had witnessed his father's transition first hand and was surrounded with aides who had a great deal of government experience. He also benefited from the leadership of Dick Cheney, who had participated in five transitions (Nixon's in 1969, Ford's in 1974, Reagan's in 1981, and George H.W. Bush's in 1989). That experience paid off. Despite a mild heart attack just two weeks after election day, Cheney played an active role as head of the transition team. He knew the importance of a good transition. "The quality of a transition has a direct bearing on the quality of the administration that follows it," he told reporters. He also knew that time was of the essence. Thus, behind-the-scenes transition planning had started immediately after election day. That is why, when the Bush team got the keys to the transition office, the president-elect was ready to name most of his cabinet members. Extensive work had already been done on lower-level appointments as well, although the sheer number of appointments that had to be confirmed by the Senate (about one thousand in all) meant that many departments would be working with barebones staff for some time to come. Still, despite all the obstacles in its path, the Bush team managed its time more efficiently and effectively than Clinton had.

A Good Start

David Gergen, himself a veteran of many Republican transitions who went on to serve in the Clinton White House, said in an interview with ABC News that the Bush team was "the most disciplined, most focused" of any since Reagan. This helped it to avoid the most serious mistakes associated with transitions. According to Charles O. Jones, these mistakes include: (1) failing to establish leadership, (2) mismanaging time and opportunity, (3) misjudging or mishandling appointments, and (4) failing to relate properly with Congress. Avoiding pitfalls in all of these areas, Bush received high marks. He reached out to members of both parties in Congress, managed his time effectively, and established leadership of the transition effort from the start.

Although several of Bush's nominees came under fire—notably his choice of John Ashcroft for attorney general—the only nomination that was derailed was that of Linda Chavez to be labor secretary, and none was clearly mishandled. Bush did expend a good deal of political capital to secure Senate confirmation of Ashcroft, but in the end the appointment helped to solidify his conservative base. The Chavez withdrawal was due to Chavez herself rather than to mishandling by the Bush team. Chavez had withheld damaging information from the new administration: an illegal Guatemalan immigrant, Marta Mercado, had lived in her home for two years. During that time Chavez paid Mercado to perform household chores. In doing so, Chavez may have violated federal laws against

A Good Start

A seasoned presidential aide praises Bush's choices for his cabinet.

President Bush has accepted his inheritance. The Bush White House staff—its policy faces all new, of course—looks, in structure and organization, very much like the staffs of preceding presidents. He has re-juggled some lines of supervision; he has created some new units; he has clearly set a new style of decorum in the place; and has set new modes of personal behavior. . . .

Good choices have indeed been made in the White House offices. The author notes with pleasure the degree of policy experience and governmental sophistication which the early contingent of Bush appointees have brought into his administration. No one, but no one, will have to remind Dick Cheney, Colin Powell, Don Rumsfeld, Condoleezza Rice, Paul O'Neill, Andy Card, or Nick Calio who is presi-

harboring and employing undocumented immigrants. The real problem, however, stemmed from the fact that Chavez not only had withheld this information but also had been at the forefront of efforts to derail Bill Clinton's nomination of Zöe Baird to be attorney general in 1993. Chavez had opposed Baird because she had hired an illegal immigrant as a nanny and had failed to pay Social Security taxes for her. At that time Chavez was sharply critical of Baird in public appearances. "I think most of the American people were upset . . . that she hired an illegal alien." Chavez said of Baird on the PBS *McNeil/Lehrer NewsHour.* "That was what upset them more than the fact that she did not pay Social Security taxes." When Chavez herself came under attack in 2001 for actions similar to Baird's, she decried the "game of search and destroy" that forced her to withdraw. Despite the embarrassment, the Bush team cut

---

dent, or will need to remonstrate them about not fighting their policy differences in public and not undermining their colleagues by leaking to their favorite columnists. These seven, in turn, have replicated the Bush *modus operandi* and have appointed many similarly experienced subordinates. While candidate Bush spoke disparagingly about "Washington" during his campaign, there was then, and there is now a welcome absence of the kind of bureaucrat-bashing which characterized the mind-set of the Reagan years.

Communication and coordination among the Bush principals have been imperfect at the beginning, but those are improvable skills which such experienced hands should quickly learn to perfect.

In these senses, a good start has been made.

Bradley H. Patterson Jr., "The New Bush White House Staff: Choices Being Made," *White House Studies*, vol. 1, Spring 2001, pp. 225–36.

its losses quickly with Chavez's withdrawal and nominated another woman for the post, Elaine Lan Chao.

The Bush Team

In the end, Bush was praised for the diversity of his cabinet and other high-level appointments. Clinton had made diversity a high priority when making appointments—so much so that it became an overriding (and ultimately distracting) theme of his transition. Bush achieved diversity with less fanfare. Clinton initially had appointed women or minorities to eight of fourteen cabinet positions: four women, three African Americans, and one Hispanic. Bush also named eight women or minorities to the cabinet: three women, two African Americans, one Hispanic, and two Asian Americans (had Chavez not withdrawn, he would have had two Hispanics and one Asian American in the cabinet). In addition, he appointed Condoleeza Rice, an African American woman, to the key post of national security adviser and Christine Todd Whitman as head of the Environmental Protection Agency. He also fulfilled his promise to name a Democrat to the cabinet—Norman Mineta as transportation secretary—and appeased both the moderate and conservative wings of his party with his other appointments.

Despite a successful transition, many observers continued to have low expectations for a Bush presidency. Could a president who came to power without winning the popular vote and after the bitter contests for Florida's electors really bring the nation together and successfully lead it—especially when that president had as little government experience as Bush? . . .

The Defining Event

Partly due to low expectations, Bush got off to a successful start in his first few weeks in office. The negative attention focused on outgoing president Bill Clinton—including concerns about his pardon of fugitive financier Marc Rich, criticism of his plans to rent expensive office space in New York City, and questions about the propriety of taking White House furniture and other gifts as he left town—also helped the new president.

Though not a great orator, Bush delivered a well-written inaugural address with poise. Inaugurations are an opportunity to bring the nation together and legitimize power relationships. Bush stressed the need for unity and civility as a way of healing the wounds of the election. . . .

Then, as the president promoted education reform in Florida on September 11, the biggest terrorist attack in U.S. history occurred in New York and the Washington area. Terrorists hijacked four U.S. passenger jets, crashing two into New York's World Trade Center and one into the Pentagon in Arlington, Virginia, across the Potomac River from the nation's capital. The fourth—presumably headed for a target in Washington—crashed in a rural part of Pennsylvania after the passengers tried to overpower the hijackers. The ensuing collapse of the trade center and the thousands of deaths caused by the terrorists galvanized the country and gave Bush his defining moment. He became, overnight, a war president.

"War has been waged against us by stealth and deceit and murder." Bush said September 14 in remarks at the National Cathedral observing the National Day of Prayer and Remembrance. "This nation is peaceful, but fierce when stirred to anger. This conflict has begun on the timing and terms of others. It will end in a way, and at an hour, of our choosing." In his weekly radio address the next day the president stressed the enormity of what lay before him: "Victory against terrorism will not take place in a single battle, but in a series of decisive actions against terrorist organizations and those who harbor and support them. We are planning a broad and sustained campaign to secure our country and eradicate the evil of terrorism."

A Changed President and Administration

President Bush's approval rating skyrocketed. A Gallup poll conducted September 13 showed it at 86 percent—up an astonishing thirty-five points in less than a week and only three points below the highest approval rating in Gallup history (89 percent for Bush's father during the Persian Gulf War). The Gallup Organization called it "the highest rally effect for any president in the past half century." Congress also rallied around the president, showing a degree of unity unprecedented in recent memory. With only one dissenting vote in the House, Congress passed a joint resolution authorizing the president to "use all necessary and appropriate force" to respond to the terrorist attacks. Congressional leaders of both parties said that they stood "shoulder-to-shoulder" with the president.

The event altered Bush's relationship with the rest of the world. The president who had seemed determined to focus on domestic problems and, in his first months in office, had sometimes been perceived as insensitive to U.S. allies, now had to build a worldwide coalition against terrorism. In remarks to reporters on September 13, Bush acknowledged that the focus of his administration had changed—waging a war on terrorism was now his first priority. In the immediate aftermath of the attacks, the world supported the United States. For the first time in its history, NATO invoked Article 5 of its charter, declaring that an attack on one member of the alliance would be considered an attack on all members. In other actions large and small, people around the world demonstrated their support for the United States: Palestinian leader Yasser Arafat gave blood, hundreds of thousands rallied at a candlelight vigil in Germany, and British officials played the "Star Spangled Banner" during the changing of the guard at Buckingham Palace.

In his remarks at the National Cathedral, Bush reminded his listeners that "adversity introduces us to ourselves." It also helped to re-introduce him to the nation.

Until then, doubts had remained about the legitimacy of his election and even about his capacity to govern. But as R.W. Apple Jr. wrote in the *New York Times*, Bush's response to the national crisis helped to change that situation: "You could almost see him growing into the clothes of the presidency." Of course, sustained leadership would be needed in the days ahead to reaffirm that newfound legitimacy. But as the president and his aides settled back to work, with Congress and the nation at least temporarily behind him—and with his political capital replenished—it seemed as if the next hundred days of his administration might count as his first.

The Bush Record Is a Mix of Noteworthy Appointments and Political Missteps

Kathryn Dunn Tenpas and Stephen Hess

In the following excerpt Kathryn Dunn Tenpas and Stephen Hess argue that Bush is to be credited for managing a smooth transition to the presidency and bringing experienced public officials to his White House. The administration is far more diverse than any previous Republican White House, and Bush avoided early miscalculations that limited the effectiveness of some of his predecessors. A tone of arrogance and costly political mistakes have dogged the administration, but Bush and his team have generally enjoyed high public support and credit for handling the war on terror with skill. Tenpas is a guest scholar, and Hess is a senior fellow at the Brookings Institution.

T HIS [EXCERPT] EXAMINES BUSH'S FIRST CRACK AT ASSEM-bling his White House and assesses its early performance, as well as the staff and structural changes made in the wake of the terrorist attacks. In an effort to gain perspective on the Bush record, we compare his staff to the initial staffs of his three immediate predecessors—Bill

Clinton, George H.W. Bush, and Ronald Reagan. More specifically, we examine appointments to the Executive Office of the President (EOP), including such senior staff members as the national security adviser and the director of the Office of Management and Budget.

The conventional wisdom was that President Bush hired an older, wiser set of advisers than President Clinton, who had rewarded "the kids"—hardworking, youthful campaign staffers. Furthermore, while Clinton worked hard to assemble a team that "looked like America," Bush hired establishment Republicans, particularly those with a conservative bent. However, staff biographies published in *National Journal* reveal remarkable similarity between the two administrations. Adding Presidents George H.W. Bush and Ronald Reagan into the comparison provides a long-term look at presidents' initial staffing, revealing additional similarities as well as important differences. . . .

Hitting the Ground Running

Seeking to avoid the missteps of the early Clinton administration as well as skepticism surrounding his ability to govern, President-elect Bush "hit the ground running." Clinton had not chosen his White House staff until a week before his inauguration. But by January 4 Bush had nearly completed the selection of his senior aides. As he made his choices public, pundits were quick to highlight distinctions between the Clinton and Bush staffs, with Bush's people clearly getting higher grades. The *National Journal*, for instance, characterized the Bush team as "one of the most experienced senior staffs in modern memory." Interestingly, the characteristics of these staffs—age, gender, ethnicity—were remarkably similar.

The average age of incoming staffers has remained steady since 1981. For all the raves about "seasoned veterans" and critiques of Clinton's youthful staff, the average age of Bush's "A" team was identical to Clinton's. Articles written in the early days of the Clinton administration portrayed his aides as "star struck young staffers" and compared the atmosphere to that of a college dormitory. The title of one op-ed piece—"Home Alone 3: The White House; Where Are the Grown ups?"—captures the sentiment among many observers. Yet for the past twenty years the average age of presidents' closest advisers has hovered in the mid-forties, a particularly productive and energetic period in the lives of many executives.

Despite opposition cries that the Bush White House is nothing but "a bunch of white males," the numbers indicate that the president appointed women and minorities in numbers that more closely resembled the composition of Clinton's White House than that of the elder Bush. Significantly, President Bush appointed women to more influential positions than any prior president. The Bush inner circle included Karen Hughes, counselor to the president ("the most powerful woman ever to work on a White House staff"), national security [adviser] Condoleezza Rice, and Margaret Spelling (née La Montagne), Assistant to the President for Domestic Policy.

President Bush's minority appointments are substantially greater than all three predecessors and, at the highest echelons, include Rice and Alberto Gonzales, counsel to the president. The expanded role of Hispanics reflects the president's Texas roots as well as the growing influence of this sector of the population.

Surrounding oneself with a home state "mafia," as the press sometimes charges, may be viewed as a president choosing loyalty over ability. But for two-term governors of the nation's two largest states, it is hardly surprising that Reagan and Bush turned to the talent pools of California and Texas for executives. The first President Bush, lacking a true home state (Connecticut, Maine, or Texas), had a low percentage of home state appointments. And despite the public impression of Washington being overrun by

Arkansans when Clinton was president, Arkansas is a very small state, which was reflected in the low number of appointments.

Defying Myths

Finally, in terms of prior experience, the Bush administration turned most often to his campaign, reflecting that there had been less "ad hocery" than in many campaign organizations. As the well-financed front-runner, he had the luxury of picking experts who could move into the White House with him. The Clinton administration was the only one in which working in the executive branch was not among the top two occupations, a phenomenon explained by the twelve-year dearth of Democratic presidents. This resulted in a smaller talent pool of former White House staff members. Working within these constraints, Clinton recruited from the halls of Congress, where Democratic aides and advisers bided their time between presidential elections.

What is most surprising in this longitudinal comparison is that much of conventional wisdom is wrong. The Clinton administration was not run by youngsters and the Bush administration was not hostile to appointing minorities and women. The realities of White House staffing defy popular myth.

His Own Stamp

Although President Bush's staff possessed qualities similar to those of his predecessors, he imposed his own ideas about running a White House by making structural changes within the EOP, reflecting his administration's priorities, goals, and general approach to governing. He began his term by adding two new units: the Office of Strategic Initiatives (OSI) and the Office of Faith-Based and Community Initiatives (OFBCI). He bolstered the Office of the Vice President, and his cabinet was given both standard and non-traditional functions. The events of September

11, 2001, additionally imposed various structural and procedural changes that affected cabinet and White House staff. Each innovation represented a break with the Clinton presidency, although in some cases there were roots in prior administrations.

The OSI, led by Bush confidant Karl Rove, was designed to think ahead and devise long-term political strategy. "It is an effort to solve the problem that consistently dogs White House staffs: the pressure to respond to unexpected events and to react to daily news cycles, which causes presidential advisers to lose sight of the big picture." The equivalent during the Reagan administration could have been the Office of Planning and Evaluation, led by Richard Beal, a colleague of pollster Richard Wirthlin. It is hardly unusual for presidents to create offices designed to ensure their political longevity. For instance, Reagan's Office of Political Affairs, initially led by Lyn Nofziger, was charged with maintaining and expanding his electoral coalition, but was not afforded the opportunity to devise long-term strategy.

The unique feature of the OSI was that the president's leading political adviser was in charge. George H.W. Bush relied on the strategic advice of Lee Atwater, but did not provide him with a White House perch. Atwater resided at the Republican National Committee until health problems forced him to resign. After Atwater's death, the absence of political insight and strategy became a serious weakness in the administration and reelection campaign. President Clinton used outside consultants James Carville, Paul Begala, Mandy Grunwald, and pollster Stanley Greenberg until the disastrous 1994 midterm elections. Subsequently, Dick Morris provided strategic input while running a consulting firm in which he offered advice to politicians of all stripes. The Bush administration clearly took a different approach by thoroughly integrating Rove into the White House chain of command. Unlike Atwater, "Rove is not content to be seen as a political operative. . . . Rove is as comfortable weighing in on trade-promotion authority as he is discussing the electoral map. . . . No other aide has Rove's singular influence on both politics and policy." The criticism of Rove is that he has over-politicized policy decisions, minimizing the input of policy expertise and maximizing the political "bang for the buck." Observers raised particular concerns over his input regarding agricultural subsidies, steel tariffs, and the pre-election saber-rattling against Iraq.

But the president's success in the 2002 midterm elections, securing Republican majorities in the House and the Senate, proved Rove's worth as a political operative. Along with Ken Mehlman, the Director of the Office of Political Affairs, Rove's OSI played an integral role in devising campaign strategy, from recruiting top-notch candidates to planning the president's appearances and fund-raising activities. Looking ahead to 2004, Karl Rove will continue to strategize and analyze the political landscape with an eye on securing the president's reelection.

Another Bush innovation, the White House OFBCI, was established by executive order. It was meant to demonstrate President Bush's commitment to "compassionate conservatism" by reaching out to faith-based and community organizations in an effort to help the needy. The initial focus of the office was the promotion of H.R. 7, a legislative initiative that sought to ease government restrictions on religious organizations so that faith-based groups could more easily provide government services, such as day care and alcohol rehabilitation. Though Republicans and Democrats alike began to question the constitutionality of financially assisting religious institutions that provide government services, the House passed the president's initiative with an anemic victory. . . .

Relying on His Team

Aside from structural innovations, President Bush expanded the influence of some positions, most notably the vice president. The stature of vice presidents has risen markedly since Jimmy Carter selected Walter Mondale in 1976, and Al Gore was clearly the most engaged vice president of the twentieth century. But Cheney's vast Washington experience, as well as his formidable role in the transition, catapulted the vice presidency to new heights. The vice president's initial activities included devising energy policy, diplomacy and congressional lobbying. In the aftermath of September 11, while intermittently placed in an "undisclosed location" for security reasons, the vice president continued to play an integral role in the administration. Cheney created the initial plan to set up the Office of Homeland Security. At the same time, his aides were fully integrated into the president's senior staff, what some describe as a "seamless operation." His chief of staff attended "most of the A-level meetings" at the White House, and two of his aides—Mary Matalin and I. Lewis Libby—also were titled assistant to the president.

In the aftermath of September 11, the administration shifted its focus to Saddam Hussein and conflict in Iraq—a shift that Cheney is thought to have precipitated. "Cheney and his small but powerful staff have emerged as the fulcrum of Bush's foreign policy. . . . Cheney's impact on the Iraq debate—or his influence on the president—cannot be overstated." Unlike his predecessors, Vice President Cheney was not assigned a particular project (e.g., global warming, reinventing government), but rather has broad-ranging influence on all manner of issues.

President Bush's reputation as one who likes to delegate authority, along with the impressive résumés of some cabinet members, led observers to expect the cabinet to play an enhanced role in the administration. According to one early forecast, "With their golden resumes, long years of public service, strong personalities and close ties to Mr. Bush, Vice President-elect Cheney, and the Republican establishment-in-waiting, the men and women of the emerging cabinet can be expected to exert just as much influence over the administration as the staff in the White House exerts, if not more." The supposition was that these department heads would need little direction from the White House, particularly on day-to-day matters. But students of American politics remembered Jimmy Carter's failed attempt to form a "cabinet government" and how his White House staff rejected this approach in favor of centralizing control, maintaining the authority to rein in cabinet members when necessary. . . .

Political Missteps

Mistakes are endemic to the start of any administration. A lethal combination of early arrogance and euphoria often derail best intentions. George W. Bush's first stumble was over the nomination of Linda Chavez to be labor secretary. Some blamed the debacle on a lax vetting process, but Chavez withdrew quickly and a less controversial successor was named and confirmed without incident. Having recovered from this mishap, a blast of criticism erupted over the delayed stock divestitures of senior staff and cabinet members, especially the holdings of treasury secretary Paul O'Neill. The heat was turned up even more when Karl Rove met with lobbyists for Intel, a company in which he owned stock, thereby opening the door to political opponents who promptly demanded an investigation. These missteps resulted in bad publicity that may have distracted White House officials but did not prove disabling.

In fact, these missteps pale in comparison with the shock waves following Senator Jim Jeffords' summer of 2001 defection from the Republican Party, causing the party's loss of majority status in the Senate, jeopardizing the president's legislative agenda, and, for the first time, casting serious doubt on the performance of the White House staff. Why didn't they know about Jeffords' apparent dissatisfaction? If they did know, why didn't they do something?

Aside from these more visible missteps, there have been various incidents that have distracted the Bush team. Among the most visible points of criticism were Vice President Cheney's reluctance to turn over energy-related documents to the General Accounting Office (GAO) and the ensuing legal battle, Attorney General Ashcroft's post–September 11 policies that have been portrayed as infringing on civil liberties, the shift away from domestic policy achievements, the eruption of corporate scandal and the congressionally motivated response, the transformation of the U.S. budget from surplus to deficit status, and the perception of the Bush team as favoring industry over the environment. Of course, no administration is beyond criticism, but the Bush team does its very best to defuse these critics. Given its approval ratings, their efforts can be deemed a success.

In addition, the Bush team has endured a steady but relatively silent stream of criticism from the press in regard to the administration's high level of secrecy. "The men and women who cover this White House believe they are being not only used, but also disrespected—and prevented from doing their jobs properly." While the relationship between president and press has always been a tense one, the danger of this "undue" level of secrecy and concomitant withholding of information may backfire if the White House should ever reach a point where some goodwill within the media is needed.

The Bush Presidency

How quickly such missteps faded in one's memory after the impressive Republican performance in the midterm elections. As we enter 2003, it is not clear that the staff and structural innovations designed to meet the challenges of "America's New War" can achieve the necessary level of integration and cooperation, but public approval ratings indicate that the perception of the Bush administration is certainly a positive one. How long this support lasts is anyone's best guess, but the instability within the economy coupled with the fallout from the conflict with Iraq could turn President Bush's numbers upside-down. Current White House staffers are all too aware of the elder Bush's last two years in office and the precipitous decline in his approval ratings. Nevertheless, the Bush team appears to have established an advisory system reflective of a unique balance between White House staff and cabinet input—a system that fits the needs of today's crisis atmosphere—with a new cabinet department taking shape in Bush's third year in office. The president will have to respond to cracks that appear in his administrative structures and personnel weaknesses and departures, but he deserves credit for diminishing the intense public fear in the aftermath of September 11 by responding in a manner that suited the needs of the country.

In the end, it is impossible for any administration to be mistake free. Stumbling is inevitable. Still, President Bush benefited from his predecessors' mistakes. His transition and first days seemed like a cakewalk compared to the unrelenting criticism faced by President Clinton. Assembling a staff of seasoned veterans in less than fifty days is no small feat. Avoiding all manner of mistakes is well beyond the realities of doing governance in Washington.

How Bush Did It

Howard Fineman

During the 2002 midterm elections, the Republican Party gained a historic victory; for the first time since 1934, a president's party was able to gain seats in both houses of Congress during his first term (the GOP gained two seats in the Senate and five seats in the House). In the following selection, Howard Fineman contends that Bush orchestrated this victory by means of a shrewd political strategy that included meticulous planning, extensive fund-raising, and effective messages. According to Fineman, this victory—along with other major triumphs—illustrates that Bush is a masterful, although underestimated political strategist. Fineman is one of the country's best known political commentators and has covered the White House and Capitol Hill as a journalist for many years.

E LECTION DAY DAWNED IN EXCELLENT FASHION FOR A president leading a war on world terror and a political campaign for control of Congress. Thanks to a well-timed leak from the Pentagon, the morning newspapers featured what amounted to a riveting, last-minute campaign ad, a story (with a dramatic picture) about how a CIA Predator drone had incinerated a carload of Al Qaeda in Yemen. By late afternoon, George W. Bush got more good news. Harvey Pitt, his gasoline-on-the-fire chairman of the SEC, had saved Bush the trouble of firing him by voluntarily resigning. With nightfall came the fun part, a dinner party upstairs in the White House, where the president would gather with allies and aides to toast his and Laura's 25th anniversary amid an elegant tableau of white candles and white roses. After dessert, they all would monitor what Karl Rove, his consigliere for 29 years, had predicted would be the happy results of a meticulously calculated Republican campaign effort, nearly two years in the making.

The chocolate cake was barely cleared when news started arriving by way of the cellular phones and pagers that Bush (who loathes them) had permitted so that Rove and his deputy, Ken Mehlman, could get returns. Republican congressional leaders watched a small TV, which was placed on a sideboard and tuned to the White House's favorite network, Fox. When word arrived early that brother Jeb had won big in Florida, Bush took a call from his father and brother in Miami, where they were celebrating family vindication. "I hope he didn't win by too much," the president joked. "I don't want to be embarrassed." He wasn't. He celebrated when the GOP saved the pivotal Colorado Senate seat, and when he got estimates that the House would not only remain in Republican hands but would add GOP seats. Bush whooped with joy when Republicans clinched Senate control by winning Missouri. By 1:20 a.m., the last of the guests were gone, Laura was asleep, but Bush (who normally goes to bed at 10) was still trolling for returns. After walking the dogs, he turned in at 2, and slept late for the first time at the White House.

By the time he awoke he was no longer the Accidental President. He was Top Gun, with (for now) the backing he needed to pursue his tough-talking vision of the war against terrorism at home and abroad. The story of his triumph has its roots in a campaign plan put into place long before 9-11, and that became an unprecedented mix of grass-roots politics, congressional policymaking and global diplomacy—each reinforcing the other in a widening gyre of power.

By last August, *Newsweek* has learned, Bush & Co. essentially had their interlocking, three-part game plan in place: to raise the stakes and lengthen the debate on our dealings with Iraq, to press the Democrats to accept the White House version of a Department of Homeland Security (and hammer them if they opposed it) and to deploy both issues to burnish the president's popularity with the GOP faithful, to whom Bush would appeal in coast-to-coast campaigning in the final weeks of the 2002 campaign.

The plan paid off. For the first time since 1934 (in FDR's first term), a president led his party to gains in both chambers of Congress two years into his first term. His Democratic opposition was left divided and confused, groping for ways to oppose a leader they had dismissed as a dimwitted usurper after the disputed election of 2000. And his domestic victory was only half of the story. Three days after the election, following two months of prodding, the U.N. Security Council unanimously supported a sternly worded resolution that gave Bush wide latitude to attack Saddam Hussein if the Iraqi dictator doesn't disarm by next February. Even Syria voted yes. "He had the equivalent of two presidencies in one week," crowed chief of staff Andy Card. "On Tuesday, he showed he is leading the country," said another top administration aide. The U.N. vote "showed he is leading the world."

The president wasted no time warning Saddam that his options were running out, and there was rising speculation in Washington about the specifics of the Pentagon assault plan, in the good chance that Iraq fails to comply with the U.N. ultimatum.

The tone was far different in domestic politics. Bush was quick to order a ban on post-election gloating, and his aides were equally quick to downplay the magnitude of the victory, noting (as did their critics) that a switch of 150,000 votes would have kept the Senate in Democratic hands. Midterm elections are comparatively low-turnout affairs, and the GOP had triumphed largely by motivating the Republican faithful, who adore Bush with an ardor unseen since the days of Ronald Reagan. A presidential election—which will require Bush to reach out to independents and even to Democrats—is another matter. "I don't want to overemphasize the volume of the shift," Rove told *Newsweek*. "The change in the American political scene is incremental and small, and our hope is that it is persistent. But we'll only know that retrospectively."

In a press conference, Bush was suitably low key, stressing the role of GOP candidates—not his own—and vowing to seek a new era of bipartisan cooperation with the Democrats as he touts legislation to create a Department of Homeland Security, to lower taxes further, deal with prescription drugs and balance the budget. As if to prove his desire for cooperation, he made a chatty phone call to Mark Pryor of Arkansas, the only Democrat to take a Senate seat from the Republicans—and Bush aides promptly distributed a picture of him making it.

The new *Newsweek* Poll illustrates why Bush should tread carefully. Despite the GOP's success, his approval rating had diminished to 60 percent, still high by historical standards but his lowest since 9-11. His "re-elect" number was 48 percent, hardly an overwhelming level as he and his aides begin to plan for the 2004 campaign. He wins a test match against Al Gore by a 54-39 percent margin, which says more about the Democrats' weakness than his own unassailability. Voters cite a prescription-drug plan for seniors as their top legislative priority—an idea that voters trust Democrats more than Republicans to implement. And by a 2-1 margin, voters want the drug plan to be run by Medicare and not, as the president prefers, by private-sector health-care providers.

Still, the magnitude of the Republicans' victory was remarkable—even if it was accomplished by overpowering a Democratic Party bereft of leadership and new ideas. The

GOP's overall vote margin in the congressional races was the largest since 1994: there were 35 million votes cast for GOP candidates, compared with 31 million for the Demo-

Helped by the War on Terrorism

Two presidential scholars contend that Bush's effectiveness in leading the war on terrorism helped secure a Republican victory in the 2002 election.

The president might have expected to have his way with Congress after the 2002 midterm elections, which increased the Republican House majority to 229 and restored the Republican Senate majority, lost when Senator James Jeffords left the Republican Party in 2001. Bush took an active role in the campaign and earned considerable credit for a party victory against the historical grain (since the Civil War, only twice before— 1934 and 1998—had the president's party picked up House seats at midterm).

September 11 and its aftermath proved enormously helpful to the Republicans in this election. Not only did Bush's leadership in the war on terrorism keep his approval ratings high, which always helps a president's party at midterm, but it also changed the focus of national politics from domestic issues, where Democrats enjoyed a popular edge, to national defense, a Republican strength. . . . President Bush was widely credited with a bold and successful strategy that effectively translated the war on terrorism and his own public standing into a solid Republican victory. With both houses of Congress in grateful Republican hands, prospects for the president's agenda looked bright.

Gary C. Jacobson and Samuel Kernell, *The Logic of American Politics in Wartime: Lessons from the Bush Administration.* Washington, DC: CQ Press, 2004, pp. 7–9.

crats. By historical standards, the GOP should have lost some 22 House seats and two Senate seats—the post–World War II average loss by a president's party in the first midterm after his election. Instead (and pending a runoff election for Senate in Louisiana), the GOP gained two seats in the Senate and five in the House. Democrats picked up some impressive governorships—in old-line industrial states such as Pennsylvania, Illinois and Michigan, and new-style industrial states such as Tennessee. But the GOP solidified its hold on the South, winning governorships in South Carolina and (for the first time in modern history) in Georgia. Rove pointed with pride to the results from the grass roots, the state legislatures. The president's party usually loses about 350 such seats in a midterm; the Republicans had netted an increase of 200, and not just in the South.

The story of how Bush pulled this off is both simple and complex, the consequence of events beyond the president's control—Al Qaeda's attack on America—and his own methodical and disciplined nature. He and Rove were quick to grasp after 9-11 that a new-era war was not only a grave challenge to the country but a political opportunity for a commander in chief and a Republican Party comfortable (in ways the Democrats generally are not) with a Manichaean view of the world and a willingness to use force as an instrument of policy.

The president's early triumphs were personal and dramatic: Bush with a bullhorn on the rubble of the Twin Towers, Bush leading the nation in prayer, Bush accepting the risk of saying "Let's roll" in Afghanistan. But these were translated into electoral and diplomatic victories last week by a process that was corporate and prosaic, the result of endless planning meetings that had all the drama of a product rollout in Cincinnati.

Long before 9-11—indeed, in the first weeks after Inauguration—GOP strategists met to plot an assault on the

Senate, which, at the time, was divided 50-50 and in their hands only by virtue of Vice President Dick Cheney's tie-breaking vote. In the winter of 2001, *Newsweek* has learned, the GOP's Senatorial Campaign Committee quietly conducted polls in 10 states with upcoming Senate races—states deemed to possess a "geographical advantage" for the party. These included "Red States" the president had won handily (among them North Carolina, Georgia and Arkansas) and those thought to be trending the GOP's way (including New Jersey and Rove's holy grail of 2002, Minnesota). More important, and more remarkably, the party secretly tested the "favorability" ratings of possible GOP contenders in those states. The idea, said Sen. Bill Frist, who heads the committee, was to be able to recruit "candidates with stature and experience." In other words, best bets.

Loyalty and ideology matter to Bush, but so does polling information. Armed with the numbers, Team Bush set about moving the chess pieces around the 2002 campaign board, clearing primary fields here, wooing reluctant entrants there. In North Carolina, *Newsweek* has learned, Frist began recruiting Elizabeth Dole (still living in Washington at the time) in the summer of 2001—barely a year after she dropped her own challenge to Bush for the GOP presidential nomination and long before the incumbent senator, Jesse Helms, announced his retirement. The White House made it clear, early and often, that Dole was its choice, avoiding what could have been a more divisive primary. Elsewhere—South Dakota is one example—Team Bush persuaded their market-tested favorite to run for the Senate; rather than for governor. Bush and Rove made a special project out of Norm Coleman in Minnesota, persuading Tim Pawlenty, who wanted to run, to seek the governorship instead.

Prodigious early fund-raising is a Bush hallmark. He was able to stomp the Republican presidential field in 2000 by amassing an unheard-of $100 million before the campaign had begun. Ditto in 2002. Bush and Cheney traveled the country through last summer, starring at fund-raisers that helped net the various Republican campaign committees record amounts of cash—$527 million, compared with $343 million for the Democrats. With extra dough, extensive polling and real-time monitoring of Democratic ad buys, the White House was able to funnel last-minute aid to down-to-the-wire Senate races—including winning GOP efforts in New Hampshire and Georgia—and away from those that weren't really close, such as Texas. The Democrats tried to do the same thing, of course, but had fewer resources and less centralized, real-time information. And they wasted valuable resources in a temporarily gratifying, but ultimately vain, effort to topple Jeb Bush.

The events of 9-11 gave the GOP an admired leader, but also a unifying, over-arching theme to run on: security. To make sure no one missed the point, Rove (and wordsmith Karen Hughes) summarized the president's postattack agenda in three parts last spring: "national security, homeland security and economic security." Rove made it clear to Republican operatives and state chairmen that, while the economy and social issues were important in the mid-terms, the party was best off relying on Bush's favorable ratings as the commander in chief and leader of the war on terror.

A genial sort, seemingly casual about details, Bush is actually a methodical executive with a penchant—almost an obsession—for planning. Last August, his inner circle gathered in Crawford, Texas, to "plan the fall," as one aide later put it. The first decision, made Aug. 8, was to keep Iraq front and center for months, not by dropping Daisy Cutters on Baghdad but by going on a long, stately march through Congress and the United Nations. Ironically, it was a course that liberal Democrats were demanding—not realizing it would be turned against them.

For the diplomatic route had multiple benefits for Bush —and the GOP. It would be easier to get congressional approval before Election Day, since many wavering Democrats hail from Red States Bush won in 2000. Holding the debate then also would focus the campaign on the president's political strength, his role as wartime leader. A congressional mandate, in turn, would give Bush more clout with the United Nations—clout that could be further amplified by victories in the midterm races. Rove, a self-taught polymath with a deep sense of history and a jeweler's eye for policy detail, participated in the planning—and knew how to best take advantage of the results: he and Mehlman put together a strenuous presidential travel schedule for the fall, though it was carefully tailored to minimize overnights on the road. "The president would have to bear the brunt if we lost, whatever he did or didn't do," Rove told *Newsweek*. "We decided that he ought to be engaged. At least that way he'd have a better chance to beat the history."

As Nov. 5 approached, Republicans unpacked an unprecedented get-out-the-vote drive called "The 72-Hour Task Force," assembled after two years of careful study of what they—and Democrats—had done well in recent elections. The answer: a back-to-the-future effort that eschewed automated phone banks in favor of personal calls and front-door visits. Big Labor, a past master of such tactics, did its best, but Democratic turnout lagged, especially among minority voters.

But what turned out to be the pivotal moment in the election came in late September, when the president and Senate Democrats failed to reach a compromise on the symbolic heart of the 2002 campaign, the homeland-security bill. Another irony: Bush initially resisted the idea of creating such a department, and had been talked into it by moderate Democrats, among them Sen. Joe Lieberman and Rep. Jane Harman. But the White House insisted on following a plan devised by former senators Warren Rudman and Gary Hart, which called for greatly limiting the role of federal employee unions in the vast new department. At least one

Democrat, Zell Miller of Georgia, wanted to go along, but Tom Daschle—under pressure from labor unions and incensed at what he saw as a cynical effort to divide his party—said no. Bush, for his part, claimed to be upset, too.

On the other hand, he and Rove had gained an issue, which they drove mercilessly. In several Red States, Democratic candidates were accused of being soft on "homeland security," their faces shown in TV ads featuring Saddam Hussein and Osama bin Laden. Often, without soothing caveats, the president said Democrats were more interested in "special interests" than the security of Americans— which left Daschle sputtering with rage. To sharpen the point, Bush began including specific examples in his final stump speeches of how Big Labor's work rules would supposedly hamper the new department's terrorist-fighting efforts. "The issue resonated," Rove said happily, adding that he credits at least two GOP wins—in Georgia and Missouri—to the Dems' defense of the unions.

Once the votes were counted, in ballot boxes and at the United Nations, Bush repaired for the weekend to Camp David. The patterns of his public life were repeating themselves, patterns established when he ran for governor of Texas and for president, and when he launched the war on terrorism with an attack on the Taliban in Afghanistan. Once again, he'd been underestimated—and exceeded expectations. Once again, he'd planned meticulously—and stuck doggedly to his game plan. Once again, he'd made few mistakes—far fewer than his enemies assumed he would. Now, at Camp David, he was back into his fitness regimen, lifting weights in the gym, jogging in the woods, even challenging his aides in bowling. There were no big meetings on the agenda, according to Card. At the Pentagon, meanwhile, Donald Rumsfeld & Co. were tinkering with their war plans. And Rove was already crunching the 2002 numbers, looking for clues. From the president's point of view, 2004 was not far away.

APPENDIX OF DOCUMENTS

Document 1: Press Conference Introducing His Education Program

One of the first acts of the new president was to introduce to the public his plan for improving failing schools, providing choice in schools through vouchers, and requiring standardized testing.

This is an important moment for my administration because I spent . . . a long amount of time campaigning on education reform. It's been the hallmark of my time as governor of Texas. My focus will be on making sure every child is educated, as the president of the United States as well.

Both parties have been talking about education reform for quite a while. It's time to come together to get it done so that we can truthfully say in America, "No child will be left behind—not one single child."

We share a moment of exceptional promise—a new administration, a newly sworn-in Congress, and we have a chance to think anew and act anew.

All of us are impatient with the old lines of division. All of us want a different attitude here in the nation's capital. All in this room, as well as across the country, know things must change.

We must confront the scandal of illiteracy in America, seen most clearly in high-poverty schools, where nearly 70 percent of fourth graders are unable to read at a basic level. We must address the low standing of America test scores amongst industrialized nations in math and science, the very subjects most likely to affect our future competitiveness. We must focus the spending of federal tax dollars on things that work. Too often we have spent without regard for results, without judging success or failure from year to year.

We must face up to the plague of school violence, with an average of 3 million crimes committed against students and teachers inside public schools every year. That's unacceptable in our country. Change will not come by adding a few new federal programs to the old. If we work only at the edges, our influence will be confined to the margins. We need real reform.

Change will not come by disdaining or dismantling the federal role of education. I believe strongly in local control of schools. I trust local folks to chart the path to excellence. But educational excellence for all is a national issue, and at this moment is a presidential priority. I've seen how real education reform can lift up scores in schools and effectively change lives.

And real education reform reflects four basic commitments. First, children must be tested every year in reading and math. Every single year. Not just in the third grade or the eighth grade, but in the third, fourth, fifth, sixth and seventh and eighth grade. I oppose a national test, one designed here in Washington, D.C., because I know it would undermine local control of schools and undermine state curricula. But states should test each student each year. Without yearly testing, we don't know who is falling behind and who needs help. Without yearly testing, too often we don't find failure until it is too late to fix. . . .

Secondly, the agents of reform must be schools and school districts, not bureaucracies. Teachers and principals, local and state leaders must have the responsibility to succeed and the flexibility to innovate. One size does not fit all when it comes to educating the children in America. School districts, school officials, educational entrepreneurs should not be hindered by excessive rules and red tape and regulation.

The principle here is a basic one. If local schools do not have the freedom to change, they cannot be held accountable for failing to change. Authority and accountability must be aligned at the local level, or schools will have a convenient excuse for failure. "I would have done it this way, but some central office or Washington, D.C., caused me to do it another way.". . .

Third, many of our schools, particularly low-income schools, will need help in the transition to higher standards. When a state sets standards, we must help schools achieve those standards. . . .

Fourth, American children must not be left in persistently dangerous or failing schools. When schools do not teach and will not change, parents and students must have other meaningful options. And when children or teenagers go to school afraid of being threatened or attacked or worst, our society must make it clear it's the ultimate betrayal of adult responsibility.

Parents and children who have only bad options must eventually get good options, if we are to succeed all across the country. There are differences of opinions about what those options should be. I made my opinion very clear in the course of the campaign, and will take my opinion to the Hill and let folks debate it. . . .

These four principles are the guides to our education reform package. Yet today I'm offering more than principles. I'm sending a series of specific proposals to the United States Congress; my own blueprint for reform. I want to begin our discussion in detail with the members of the House and the Senate, because I know we need to act by this summer so that the people at the local level can take our initiatives and plan for the school year beginning next fall.

I'm going to listen to suggestions from folks. If somebody's got a better idea, I hope they bring it forward, because the secretary and I will listen.

We've got one thing in mind: an education system that's responsive to the children, an education system that educates every child, an education system that I'm confident can exist; one that's based upon sound fundamental curriculum, one that starts teaching children to read early in life, one that focuses on systems that do work, one that heralds our teachers and makes sure they've got the necessary tools to teach, but one that says every child can learn. And in this great land called America, no child will be left behind.

George W. Bush, press conference to introduce the president's education program, January 23, 2001.

Document 2: Radio Address on the Economy

President Bush addressed the nation early into his presidency to introduce his economic plan. His tax relief proposal was sent to Congress the week after this address.

This coming week I will send to Congress my tax relief plan. It is broad and responsible. It will help our economy, and it is the right thing to do.

Today many Americans are feeling squeezed. They work 40, 50, 60 hours a week, and still have trouble paying the electric bill and the grocery bill at the same time. At the end of a long week, they collect their paycheck, and what the federal government takes is often unfair.

Picture a diner in one of our cities. At the table is a lawyer with two children. She earns $250,000 a year. Carrying her coffee and toast is a waitress who has two children of her own. She earns $25,000 a year. If both the lawyer and the waitress get a raise, it is the waitress who winds up paying a higher marginal tax rate. She will give back almost half of every extra dollar she earns to the government.

Both of these women, the lawyer and the waitress, deserve a tax cut. Under my plan, both of these women, and all Americans who pay taxes will get one. For the waitress, our plan will wipe out her income tax bill entirely.

My plan does some important things for America. It reduces taxes for everyone who pays taxes. It lowers the lowest income tax rate from

15 percent to 10 percent. It cuts the highest rate to 33 percent, because I believe no one should pay more than a third of their income to the federal government. The average family of four will get about $1,600 of their own money returned back to them.

There's a lot of talk in Washington about paying down the national debt, and that's good, and that's important. And my budget will do that. But American families have debts to pay, as well. A tax cut now will stimulate our economy and create jobs.

The economic news these days is troubling—rising energy prices, layoffs, falling consumer confidence. This is not a time for government to be taking more money than it needs away from the people who buy goods and create jobs.

My plan will keep all Social Security money in the Social Security system, where it belongs. We will eliminate the death tax, saving family farms and family-owned businesses. We'll reduce the maximum rate on small business income to 33 percent, so they can help create the jobs we need. Above all, my plan unlocks the door to the middle class for millions of hardworking Americans.

The country has prospered mightily over the past 20 years. But a lot of people feel as if they have been looking through the window at somebody else's party. It is time to fling those doors and windows open and invite everybody in. It is time to reward the work of people trying to enter the middle class and put some more money in their pockets at a time when they need it.

My tax reduction plan does all these things, and I hope you'll support it.

George W. Bush, radio address to the nation, February 3, 2001.

Document 3: Statement Following the September 11 Attacks

Bush's first detailed response to the terrorist attacks reflects his faith and determination.

Today, our fellow citizens, our way of life, our very freedom came under attack in a series of deliberate and deadly terrorist acts. The victims were in airplanes, or in their offices; secretaries, businessmen and women, military and federal workers; moms and dads, friends and neighbors. Thousands of lives were suddenly ended by evil, despicable acts of terror.

The pictures of airplanes flying into buildings, fires burning, huge structures collapsing, have filled us with disbelief, terrible sadness, and a quiet, unyielding anger. These acts of mass murder were intended to frighten our nation into chaos and retreat. But they have failed; our country is strong.

A great people has been moved to defend a great nation. Terrorist attacks can shake the foundations of our biggest buildings, but they cannot touch the foundation of America. These acts shattered steel, but they cannot dent the steel of American resolve.

America was targeted for attack because we're the brightest beacon for freedom and opportunity in the world. And no one will keep that light from shining.

Today, our nation saw evil, the very worst of human nature. And we responded with the best of America—with the daring of our rescue workers, with the caring for strangers and neighbors who came to give blood and help in any way they could.

Immediately following the first attack, I implemented our government's emergency response plans. Our military is powerful, and it's prepared. Our emergency teams are working in New York City and Washington, D.C., to help with local rescue efforts.

Our first priority is to get help to those who have been injured, and to take every precaution to protect our citizens at home and around the world from further attacks.

The functions of our government continue without interruption. Federal agencies in Washington which had to be evacuated today are reopening for essential personnel tonight, and will be open for business tomorrow. Our financial institutions remain strong, and the American economy will be open for business, as well.

The search is underway for those who are behind these evil acts. I've directed the full resources of our intelligence and law enforcement communities to find those responsible and to bring them to justice. We will make no distinction between the terrorists who committed these acts and those who harbor them.

I appreciate so very much the members of Congress who have joined me in strongly condemning these attacks. And on behalf of the American people, I thank the many world leaders who have called to offer their condolences and assistance.

America and our friends and allies join with all those who want peace and security in the world, and we stand together to win the war against terrorism. Tonight, I ask for your prayers for all those who grieve, for the children whose worlds have been shattered, for all whose sense of safety and security has been threatened. And I pray they will be comforted by a power greater than any of us, spoken through the ages in Psalm 23: "Even though I walk through the valley of the shadow of death, I fear no evil, for You are with me."

This is a day when all Americans from every walk of life unite in our resolve for justice and peace. America has stood down enemies before, and we will do so this time. None of us will ever forget this day. Yet, we go forward to defend freedom and all that is good and just in our world.

George W. Bush, statement to the nation, September 11, 2001.

Document 4: Second State of the Union Address

Bush summarizes his efforts in the war on terror and discusses his plans for the future in his second State of the Union Address, his first following the September 11, 2001, terrorist attacks. He vows to oppose "the axis of evil," the states that threaten America with terrorism.

As we gather tonight, our nation is at war, our economy is in recession, and the civilized world faces unprecedented dangers. Yet the state of our Union has never been stronger.

We last met in an hour of shock and suffering. In four short months, our nation has comforted the victims, begun to rebuild New York and the Pentagon, rallied a great coalition, captured, arrested, and rid the world of thousands of terrorists, destroyed Afghanistan's terrorist training camps, saved a people from starvation, and freed a country from brutal oppression.

The American flag flies again over our embassy in Kabul. Terrorists who once occupied Afghanistan now occupy cells at Guantanamo Bay. And terrorist leaders who urged followers to sacrifice their lives are running for their own. . . .

Our progress is a tribute to the spirit of the Afghan people, to the resolve of our coalition, and to the might of the United States military. When I called our troops into action, I did so with complete confidence in their courage and skill. And tonight, thanks to them, we are winning the war on terror. The men and women of our Armed Forces have delivered a message now clear to every enemy of the United States: Even 7,000 miles away, across oceans and continents, on mountaintops and in caves—you will not escape the justice of this nation. . . .

Our cause is just, and it continues. Our discoveries in Afghanistan confirmed our worst fears, and showed us the true scope of the task ahead. We have seen the depth of our enemies' hatred in videos, where they laugh about the loss of innocent life. And the depth of their hatred is equaled by the madness of the destruction they design. We have found diagrams of American nuclear power plants and public water facilities, detailed instructions for making chemical weapons, surveillance maps of American cities, and thorough descriptions of land-marks in America and throughout the world.

What we have found in Afghanistan confirms that, far from ending there, our war against terror is only beginning. Most of the 19 men who hijacked planes on September the 11th were trained in Afghanistan's camps, and so were tens of thousands of others. Thousands of dangerous killers, schooled in the methods of murder, often supported by outlaw regimes, are now spread throughout the world like ticking time bombs, set to go off without warning.

Thanks to the work of our law enforcement officials and coalition partners, hundreds of terrorists have been arrested. Yet, tens of thousands of trained terrorists are still at large. These enemies view the entire world as a battlefield, and we must pursue them wherever they are. So long as training camps operate, so long as nations harbor terrorists, freedom is at risk. And America and our allies must not, and will not, allow it.

Our nation will continue to be steadfast and patient and persistent in the pursuit of two great objectives. First, we will shut down terrorist camps, disrupt terrorist plans, and bring terrorists to justice. And, second, we must prevent the terrorists and regimes who seek chemical, biological or nuclear weapons from threatening the United States and the world.

Our military has put the terror training camps of Afghanistan out of business, yet camps still exist in at least a dozen countries. A terrorist underworld—including groups like Hamas, Hezbollah, Islamic Jihad, Jaish-i-Mohammed—operates in remote jungles and deserts, and hides in the centers of large cities.

While the most visible military action is in Afghanistan, America is acting elsewhere. We now have troops in the Philippines, helping to train that country's armed forces to go after terrorist cells that have executed an American, and still hold hostages. Our soldiers, working with the Bosnian government, seized terrorists who were plotting to bomb our embassy. Our Navy is patrolling the coast of Africa to block the shipment of weapons and the establishment of terrorist camps in Somalia.

My hope is that all nations will heed our call, and eliminate the terrorist parasites who threaten their countries and our own. Many nations are acting forcefully. Pakistan is now cracking down on terror, and I admire the strong leadership of President Musharraf.

But some governments will be timid in the face of terror. And make no mistake about it: If they do not act, America will.

Our second goal is to prevent regimes that sponsor terror from threatening America or our friends and allies with weapons of mass destruction. Some of these regimes have been pretty quiet since September the 11th. But we know their true nature. North Korea is a regime arming with missiles and weapons of mass destruction, while starving its citizens.

Iran aggressively pursues these weapons and exports terror, while an unelected few repress the Iranian people's hope for freedom.

Iraq continues to flaunt its hostility toward America and to support terror. The Iraqi regime has plotted to develop anthrax, and nerve gas, and nuclear weapons for over a decade. This is a regime that has already used poison gas to murder thousands of its own citizens—leaving the bodies of mothers huddled over their dead children. This is a regime that agreed to international inspections—then kicked out the inspectors. This is a regime that has something to hide from the civilized world.

States like these, and their terrorist allies, constitute an axis of evil, arming to threaten the peace of the world. By seeking weapons of mass destruction, these regimes pose a grave and growing danger. They could provide these arms to terrorists, giving them the means to match their hatred. They could attack our allies or attempt to blackmail the United States. In any of these cases, the price of indifference would be catastrophic.

We will work closely with our coalition to deny terrorists and their state sponsors the materials, technology, and expertise to make and deliver weapons of mass destruction. We will develop and deploy effective missile defenses to protect America and our allies from sudden attack. And all nations should know: America will do what is necessary to ensure our nation's security.

We'll be deliberate, yet time is not on our side. I will not wait on events, while dangers gather. I will not stand by, as peril draws closer and closer. The United States of America will not permit the world's most dangerous regimes to threaten us with the world's most destructive weapons.

Our war on terror is well begun, but it is only begun. This campaign may not be finished on our watch—yet it must be and it will be waged on our watch.

We can't stop short. If we stop now—leaving terror camps intact and terror states unchecked—our sense of security would be false and temporary. History has called America and our allies to action, and it is both our responsibility and our privilege to fight freedom's fight.

Our first priority must always be the security of our nation, and that will be reflected in the budget I send to Congress. My budget supports three great goals for America: We will win this war; we'll protect our homeland; and we will revive our economy.

September the 11th brought out the best in America, and the best in this Congress. And I join the American people in applauding your unity and resolve. Now Americans deserve to have this same spirit directed toward addressing problems here at home. I'm a proud member of my party—yet as we act to win the war, protect our people, and create jobs in America, we must act, first and foremost, not as Republicans, not as Democrats, but as Americans. . . .

The last time I spoke here, I expressed the hope that life would return to normal. In some ways, it has. In others, it never will. Those of us who have lived through these challenging times have been changed by them. We've come to know truths that we will never question: evil is real, and it must be opposed. Beyond all differences of race or creed, we are one country, mourning together and facing danger together. Deep in the American character, there is honor, and it is stronger than cynicism. And many have discovered again that even in tragedy—especially in tragedy—God is near.

In a single instant, we realized that this will be a decisive decade in the history of liberty, that we've been called to a unique role in human events. Rarely has the world faced a choice more clear or consequential.

Our enemies send other people's children on missions of suicide and murder. They embrace tyranny and death as a cause and a creed. We stand for a different choice, made long ago, on the day of our founding. We affirm it again today. We choose freedom and the dignity of every life.

Steadfast in our purpose, we now press on. We have known freedom's price. We have shown freedom's power. And in this great conflict, my fellow Americans, we will see freedom's victory.

Thank you all. May God bless.

George W. Bush, State of the Union Address, January 29, 2002.

Document 5: Address to the United Nations on Iraq

Bush addressed the United Nations in an effort to gain support for U.S. efforts to remove the regime of Saddam Hussein. Bush's speech is credited with prompting the UN Security Council to unanimously pass Resolution 1441, which called on Iraq to disarm.

Our principles and our security are challenged today by outlaw groups and regimes that accept no law of morality and have no limit to their violent ambitions. In the attacks on America a year ago, we saw the destructive intentions of our enemies. This threat hides within many nations, including my own. In cells and camps, terrorists are plotting further destruction, and building new bases for their war against civilization. And our greatest fear is that terrorists will find a shortcut to their mad ambitions when an outlaw regime supplies them with the technologies to kill on a massive scale.

In one place—in one regime—we find all these dangers, in their most lethal and aggressive forms, exactly the kind of aggressive threat the United Nations was born to confront.

Twelve years ago, Iraq invaded Kuwait without provocation. And the regime's forces were poised to continue their march to seize other countries and their resources. Had Saddam Hussein been appeased instead of stopped, he would have endangered the peace and stability of the world. Yet this aggression was stopped—by the might of coalition forces and the will of the United Nations.

To suspend hostilities, to spare himself, Iraq's dictator accepted a series of commitments. The terms were clear, to him and to all. And he agreed to prove he is complying with every one of those obligations.

He has proven instead only his contempt for the United Nations, and for all his pledges. By breaking every pledge—by his deceptions, and by his cruelties—Saddam Hussein has made the case against himself.

In 1991, Security Council Resolution 688 demanded that the Iraqi regime cease at once the repression of its own people, including the systematic repression of minorities—which the Council said, threatened international peace and security in the region. This demand goes ignored.

Last year, the U.N. Commission on Human Rights found that Iraq continues to commit extremely grave violations of human rights, and that the regime's repression is all pervasive. Tens of thousands of political opponents and ordinary citizens have been subjected to arbitrary arrest and imprisonment, summary execution, and torture by beating and burning, electric shock, starvation, mutilation, and rape. Wives are tortured in front of their husbands, children in the presence of their parents—and all of these horrors concealed from the world by the apparatus of a totalitarian state.

In 1991, the U.N. Security Council, through Resolutions 686 and 687, demanded that Iraq return all prisoners from Kuwait and other lands. Iraq's regime agreed. It broke its promise. Last year the Secretary General's high-level coordinator for this issue reported that Kuwait, Saudi, Indian, Syrian, Lebanese, Iranian, Egyptian, Bahraini, and Omani nationals remain unaccounted for—more than 600 people. One American pilot is among them.

In 1991, the U.N. Security Council, through Resolution 687, demanded that Iraq renounce all involvement with terrorism, and permit no terrorist organizations to operate in Iraq. Iraq's regime agreed. It broke this promise. In violation of Security Council Resolution 1373, Iraq continues to shelter and support terrorist organizations that direct violence against Iran, Israel, and Western governments. Iraqi dissidents abroad are targeted for murder. In 1993, Iraq attempted to assassinate the Emir of Kuwait and a former American President. Iraq's government openly praised the attacks of September the 11th. And al Qaeda terrorists escaped from Afghanistan and are known to be in Iraq.

In 1991, the Iraqi regime agreed to destroy and stop developing all weapons of mass destruction and long-range missiles, and to prove to the world it has done so by complying with rigorous inspections. Iraq has broken every aspect of this fundamental pledge.

From 1991 to 1995, the Iraqi regime said it had no biological weapons. After a senior official in its weapons program defected and exposed this lie, the regime admitted to producing tens of thousands of liters of anthrax and other deadly biological agents for use with Scud warheads, aerial bombs, and aircraft spray tanks. U.N. inspectors believe Iraq has produced two to four times the amount of biological agents it declared, and has failed to account for more than three metric tons of material that could be used to produce biological weapons. Right now, Iraq is expanding and improving facilities that were used for the production of biological weapons.

United Nations' inspections also revealed that Iraq likely maintains stockpiles of VX, mustard and other chemical agents, and that the regime is rebuilding and expanding facilities capable of producing chemical weapons.

And in 1995, after four years of deception, Iraq finally admitted it had a crash nuclear weapons program prior to the Gulf War. We know now, were it not for that war, the regime in Iraq would likely have possessed a nuclear weapon no later than 1993.

Today, Iraq continues to withhold important information about its nuclear program—weapons design, procurement logs, experiment data, an accounting of nuclear materials and documentation of foreign assistance.

Iraq employs capable nuclear scientists and technicians. It retains physical infrastructure needed to build a nuclear weapon. Iraq has made several attempts to buy high-strength aluminum tubes used to enrich uranium for a nuclear weapon. Should Iraq acquire fissile material, it would be able to build a nuclear weapon within a year. And Iraq's state-controlled media has reported numerous meetings between Saddam Hussein and his nuclear scientists, leaving little doubt about his continued appetite for these weapons.

Iraq also possesses a force of Scud-type missiles with ranges beyond the 150 kilometers permitted by the U.N. Work at testing and production facilities shows that Iraq is building more long-range missiles that it can inflict mass death throughout the region.

In 1990, after Iraq's invasion of Kuwait, the world imposed economic sanctions on Iraq. Those sanctions were maintained after the war to compel the regime's compliance with Security Council resolutions. In time, Iraq was allowed to use oil revenues to buy food. Saddam Hussein has subverted this program, working around the sanctions to buy missile technology and military materials. He blames the suffering of Iraq's people on the United Nations, even as he uses his oil wealth to build lavish palaces for himself, and to buy arms for his country. By refusing to comply with his own agreements, he bears full guilt for the hunger and misery of innocent Iraqi citizens.

In 1991, Iraq promised U.N. inspectors immediate and unrestricted access to verify Iraq's commitment to rid itself of weapons of mass destruction and long-range missiles. Iraq broke this promise, spending seven years deceiving, evading, and harassing U.N. inspectors before ceasing cooperation entirely. Just months after the 1991 cease-fire, the Security Council twice renewed its demand that the Iraqi regime cooperate fully with inspectors, condemning Iraq's serious violations of its obligations. The Security Council again renewed that demand in 1994, and twice more in 1996, deploring Iraq's clear violations of its obligations. The Security Council renewed its demand three more times in 1997, citing flagrant violations; and three more times in 1998, calling Iraq's behavior totally unacceptable. And in 1999, the demand was renewed yet again.

As we meet today, it's been almost four years since the last U.N. inspectors set foot in Iraq, four years for the Iraqi regime to plan, and to build, and to test behind the cloak of secrecy.

We know that Saddam Hussein pursued weapons of mass murder even when inspectors were in his country. Are we to assume that he stopped when they left? The history, the logic, and the facts lead to one conclusion: Saddam Hussein's regime is a grave and gathering danger. To suggest otherwise is to hope against the evidence. To assume this regime's good faith is to bet the lives of millions and the peace of the world in a reckless gamble. And this is a risk we must not take.

Delegates to the General Assembly, we have been more than patient. We've tried sanctions. We've tried the carrot of oil for food, and the stick of coalition military strikes. But Saddam Hussein has defied all these efforts and continues to develop weapons of mass destruction. The first time we may be completely certain he has a—nuclear weapons is when, God forbids, he uses one. We owe it to all our citizens to do everything in our power to prevent that day from coming.

George W. Bush, remarks at the UN General Assembly, September 12, 2002.

Document 6: National Security Strategy of the United States

In his introduction to the new national security plans for the United States, Bush announces his doctrine of preemption (subsequently known as the "Bush Doctrine"), whereby he pledges to take action against those who threaten the United States before they can attack the country.

The great struggles of the twentieth century between liberty and totalitarianism ended with a decisive victory for the forces of freedom— and a single sustainable model for national success: freedom, democracy, and free enterprise. In the twenty-first century, only nations that share a commitment to protecting basic human rights and guaranteeing political and economic freedom will be able to unleash the potential of their people and assure their future prosperity. People everywhere want to be able to speak freely; choose who will govern them; worship as they please; educate their children—male and female; own property; and enjoy the benefits of their labor. These values of freedom are right and true for every person, in every society—and the duty of protecting these values against their enemies is the common calling of freedom-loving people across the globe and across the ages.

Today, the United States enjoys a position of unparalleled military strength and great economic and political influence. In keeping with our heritage and principles, we do not use our strength to press for unilateral advantage. We seek instead to create a balance of power that favors human freedom: conditions in which all nations and all societies can choose for themselves the rewards and challenges of political and economic liberty. In a world that is safe, people will be able to make their own lives better. We will defend the peace by fighting terrorists and tyrants. We will preserve the peace by building good relations among the great powers. We will extend the peace by encouraging free and open societies on every continent.

Defending our Nation against its enemies is the first and fundamental commitment of the Federal Government. Today, that task has changed dramatically. Enemies in the past needed great armies and great industrial capabilities to endanger America. Now, shadowy networks of individuals can bring great chaos and suffering to our shores for less than it costs to purchase a single tank. Terrorists are organized to penetrate open societies and to turn the power of modern technologies against us.

To defeat this threat we must make use of every tool in our arsenal—military power, better homeland defenses, law enforcement, intelligence, and vigorous efforts to cut off terrorist financing. The war against terrorists of global reach is a global enterprise of uncertain duration. America will help nations that need our assistance in combating terror. And America will hold to account nations that are compromised by terror, including those who harbor terrorists—because the allies of terror are the enemies of civilization. The United States and countries cooperating with us must not allow the terrorists to develop new home bases. Together, we will seek to deny them sanctuary at every turn.

The gravest danger our Nation faces lies at the crossroads of radicalism and technology. Our enemies have openly declared that they are seeking weapons of mass destruction, and evidence indicates that they are doing so with determination. The United States will not allow these efforts to succeed. We will build defenses against ballistic missiles and other means of delivery. We will cooperate with other nations to deny, contain, and curtail our enemies' efforts to acquire dangerous technologies. And, as a matter of common sense and self-defense, America will act against such emerging threats before they are fully formed. We cannot defend America and our friends by hoping for the best. So we must be prepared to defeat our enemies' plans, using the best intelligence and proceeding with deliberation. History will judge harshly those who saw this coming danger but failed to act. In the new world we have entered, the only path to peace and security is the path of action.

As we defend the peace, we will also take advantage of an historic opportunity to preserve the peace. Today, the international community has the best chance since the rise of the nation-state in the seventeenth century to build a world where great powers compete in peace instead of continually prepare for war. Today, the world's great powers find ourselves on the same side—united by common dangers of terrorist violence and chaos. The United States will build on these common interests to promote global security. We are also increasingly united by common values. Russia is in the midst of a hopeful transition, reaching for its democratic future and a partner in the war on terror. Chinese leaders are discovering that economic freedom is the only source of national wealth. In time, they will find that social and political freedom is the only source of national greatness. America will encourage the advancement of democracy and economic openness in both nations, because these are the best foundations for domestic stability and international order. We will strongly resist aggression from other great powers—even as we welcome their peaceful pursuit of prosperity, trade, and cultural advancement.

Finally, the United States will use this moment of opportunity to extend the benefits of freedom across the globe. We will actively work to bring the hope of democracy, development, free markets, and free trade to every corner of the world. The events of September 11, 2001, taught us that weak states, like Afghanistan, can pose as great a danger to our national interests as strong states. Poverty does not make poor people into terrorists and murderers. Yet poverty, weak institutions, and corruption can make weak states vulnerable to terrorist networks and drug cartels within their borders.

The United States will stand beside any nation determined to build a better future by seeking the rewards of liberty for its people. Free trade and free markets have proven their ability to lift whole societies out of poverty—so the United States will work with individual nations, entire regions, and the entire global trading community to build a world that trades in freedom and therefore grows in prosperity. The United States will deliver greater development assistance through the New Millennium Challenge Account to nations that govern justly, invest in their people, and encourage economic freedom. We will also continue to lead the world in efforts to reduce the terrible toll of HIV/AIDS and other infectious diseases.

In building a balance of power that favors freedom, the United States is guided by the conviction that all nations have important responsibilities. Nations that enjoy freedom must actively fight terror. Nations that depend on international stability must help prevent the spread of weapons of mass destruction. Nations that seek international aid must govern themselves wisely, so that aid is well spent. For freedom to thrive, accountability must be expected and required.

We are also guided by the conviction that no nation can build a safer, better world alone. Alliances and multilateral institutions can multiply the strength of freedom-loving nations. The United States is committed to lasting institutions like the United Nations, the World Trade Organization, the Organization of American States, and NATO as well as other long-standing alliances. Coalitions of the willing can augment these permanent institutions. In all cases, international obligations are to be taken seriously. They are not to be undertaken symbolically to rally support for an ideal without furthering its attainment.

Freedom is the non-negotiable demand of human dignity; the birthright of every person—in every civilization. Throughout history, freedom has been threatened by war and terror; it has been challenged by the clashing wills of powerful states and the evil designs of tyrants; and it has been tested by widespread poverty and disease. Today, humanity holds in its hands the opportunity to further freedom's triumph over all these foes. The United States welcomes our responsibility to lead in this great mission.

George W. Bush, *The National Security Strategy of the United States of America.* Washington, DC: White House Press Office, 2002.

Document 7: White House Briefing on the Anniversary of No Child Left Behind

In a White House briefing from the East Room, President Bush celebrates the one-year anniversary of his education plan.

This is an interesting day; it marks the anniversary of an incredibly important legislative accomplishment. It was a year ago that I signed the No Child Left Behind Education Act. It was the most meaningful education reform probably ever. . . .

It was a legislative victory on behalf of the children of America. And it showed the American people that when people set aside this needless partisan bickering, we can get some positive things done.

So, a year ago we signed the piece of legislation that I'm absolutely confident is going to change our schools for the better; change the whole structure of education for the good. But it also was a signal to those who love to divide in Washington, D.C. that when we put our minds to it, when we focus on the greater good, we can get a lot done.

So I want to congratulate the members of both political parties, on this anniversary, for working so hard to accomplish a significant and meaningful piece of legislation. And now we've got to get to work. Now we got to do the job that's expected.

We can say that the work of reform is well begun. And that's . . . a true statement. The work will be complete, however, when every school, every public school in America is a place of high expectations and a place of achievement.

That is our national goal. . . .

Many schools in our country are places of hope and opportunity.

... Unfortunately, too many schools in America have failed in that mission. The harm has been greatest in the poor and minority communities. Those kids have been hurt the worst because people have failed to challenge the soft bigotry of low expectations.

Over the years, parents across America have heard a lot of excuses—that's a reality—and oftentimes have seen little change. One year ago today, the time for excuse-making has come to an end. With the No Child Left Behind Act, we have committed the nation to higher standards for every single public school, and we have committed the resources to help the students achieve those standards. We affirm the right of parents to have better information about the schools, and to make crucial decisions about their children's future.

Accountability for results is no longer just a hope of parents; accountability for results is now the law of the land. In return for receiving federal money, states must design accountability systems to measure whether students are learning to read and write and add and subtract. In return for a lot of money, the federal government, for the first time, is asking—Are we getting the kind of return the American people want for every child? The only way to be sure of whether or not every child is learning is to test regularly and to show everybody, especially the parents, the results of the tests.

The law further requires that test scores be presented in a clear and meaningful way, so that we can find the learning problems within each group of students. I'll show off a little bit—it's called disaggregation of results.

Annual report cards are required to grade the schools themselves, so parents can judge how the schools compare to others. Excellence will be recognized. It's so important for us to measure, so that we can praise the principals and teachers who are accomplishing the objectives we all hope for.

And at the same time, poor performance cannot be disguised or hidden. Schools that perform poorly will be noticeable, and given time and given incentives and given resources to improve. Schools that don't improve will begin to face consequences, such as that parents can move their child to another public school, or hire a tutor or any other academic help. We will not accept a school that does not teach and will not change.

Schools have a responsibility to improve, and they also have the freedom to improve in this law, and that's important. I can assure you I haven't changed my attitude about federal control of schools. When I was the governor of Texas, I didn't like the idea of federal control of schools. I felt we were pretty competent in the state of Texas to run our own schools. I still feel that way, now that I've been up here for two years. I believe in local control of schools.

And this principle is inherent in this bill. The key choices about curriculum and teaching methods will be made at the state and local level. Input will be given by parents and teachers and principals, who know the local culture best. Parents and educators will not be bystanders in education reform. As a matter of fact, in our view, they are the agents of education reform. And this law upholds that principle as well. . . .

One year ago, we met the first challenge of education reform. We passed a law. And now we've got another challenge, and that's the implementation of this law. Today, we honor five states; there are 45 more to go. Some of the education leaders of those states are here. We look forward to seeing your plans. We look forward to seeing the spirit of the No Child Left Behind law in your plans. We look forward to strong accountability systems. We look forward to seeing the implementation of curricula that works. We look forward to the hiring of principals who know how to lead a school. We look forward to rewarding teachers who are not only lending their hearts, but their talents to make sure no child gets left behind. We look forward to a culture in America that understands every child can learn. And we look forward to the day that no child in this country is ever left behind.

George W. Bush, remarks on the anniversary of the No Child Left Behind Act, January 8, 2003.

Document 8: Announcement of War with Iraq

Bush announces the start of the invasion of Iraq and frames the conflict in the context of defending the world from "grave danger." He also describes the invasion as a coalition effort.

My fellow citizens, at this hour, American and coalition forces are in the early stages of military operations to disarm Iraq, to free its people and to defend the world from grave danger.

On my orders, coalition forces have begun striking selected targets of military importance to undermine Saddam Hussein's ability to wage war. These are opening stages of what will be a broad and concerted campaign. More than 35 countries are giving crucial support— from the use of naval and air bases, to help with intelligence and logistics, to the deployment of combat units. Every nation in this coalition has chosen to bear the duty and share the honor of serving in our common defense.

To all the men and women of the United States Armed Forces now in the Middle East, the peace of a troubled world and the hopes of an oppressed people now depend on you. That trust is well placed.

The enemies you confront will come to know your skill and bravery. The people you liberate will witness the honorable and decent spirit of the American military. In this conflict, America faces an enemy who has no regard for conventions of war or rules of morality. Saddam Hussein has placed Iraqi troops and equipment in civilian areas, attempting to use innocent men, women and children as shields for his own military—a final atrocity against his people.

I want Americans and all the world to know that coalition forces will make every effort to spare innocent civilians from harm. A campaign on the harsh terrain of a nation as large as California could be longer and more difficult than some predict. And helping Iraqis achieve a united, stable and free country will require our sustained commitment.

We come to Iraq with respect for its citizens, for their great civilization and for the religious faiths they practice. We have no ambition in Iraq, except to remove a threat and restore control of that country to its own people.

I know that the families of our military are praying that all those who serve will return safely and soon. Millions of Americans are praying with you for the safety of your loved ones and for the protection of the innocent. For your sacrifice, you have the gratitude and respect of the American people. And you can know that our forces will be coming home as soon as their work is done.

Our nation enters this conflict reluctantly—yet, our purpose is sure. The people of the United States and our friends and allies will not live at the mercy of an outlaw regime that threatens the peace with weapons of mass murder. We will meet that threat now, with our Army, Air Force, Navy, Coast Guard and Marines, so that we do not have to meet it later with armies of fire fighters and police and doctors on the streets of our cities.

Now that conflict has come, the only way to limit its duration is to apply decisive force. And I assure you, this will not be a campaign of half measures, and we will accept no outcome but victory.

My fellow citizens, the dangers to our country and the world will be overcome. We will pass through this time of peril and carry on the work of peace. We will defend our freedom. We will bring freedom to others and we will prevail.

May God bless our country and all who defend her.

George W. Bush, address to the nation, March 19, 2003.

Document 9: Declaration of the End of Major Combat Operations in Iraq

In a speech from the deck of the aircraft carrier the USS Abraham Lincoln, *Bush announces an end to major combat missions in Iraq.*

Admiral Kelly, Captain Card, officers and sailors of the USS *Abraham Lincoln*, my fellow Americans: Major combat operations in Iraq have ended. In the battle of Iraq, the United States and our allies have prevailed. And now our coalition is engaged in securing and reconstructing that country.

In this battle, we have fought for the cause of liberty, and for the peace of the world. Our nation and our coalition are proud of this accomplishment—yet, it is you, the members of the United States military, who achieved it. Your courage, your willingness to face danger for your country and for each other, made this day possible. Because of you, our nation is more secure. Because of you, the tyrant has fallen, and Iraq is free.

Operation Iraqi Freedom was carried out with a combination of precision and speed and boldness the enemy did not expect, and the world had not seen before. From distant bases or ships at sea, we sent planes and missiles that could destroy an enemy division, or strike a single bunker. Marines and soldiers charged to Baghdad across 350 miles of hostile ground, in one of the swiftest advances of heavy arms in history. You have shown the world the skill and the might of the American Armed Forces.

This nation thanks all the members of our coalition who joined in a noble cause. We thank the Armed Forces of the United Kingdom, Australia, and Poland, who shared in the hardships of war. We thank all the citizens of Iraq who welcomed our troops and joined in the liberation of their own country. And tonight, I have a special word for Secretary Rumsfeld, for General Franks, and for all the men and women who wear the uniform of the United States: America is grateful for a job well done.

The character of our military through history—the daring of Normandy, the fierce courage of Iwo Jima, the decency and idealism that turned enemies into allies—is fully present in this generation. When Iraqi civilians looked into the faces of our servicemen and women, they saw strength and kindness and goodwill. When I look at the members of the United States military, I see the best of our country, and I'm honored to be your Commander-in-Chief.

In the images of falling statues, we have witnessed the arrival of a new era. For a hundred of years of war, culminating in the nuclear age, military technology was designed and deployed to inflict casualties on an ever-growing scale. In defeating Nazi Germany and Imperial Japan, Allied forces destroyed entire cities, while enemy leaders who started the conflict were safe until the final days. Military power was used to end a regime by breaking a nation.

Today, we have the greater power to free a nation by breaking a dangerous and aggressive regime. With new tactics and precision weapons, we can achieve military objectives without directing violence against civilians. No device of man can remove the tragedy from war; yet it is a great moral advance when the guilty have far more to fear from war than the innocent.

In the images of celebrating Iraqis, we have also seen the ageless appeal of human freedom. Decades of lies and intimidation could not make the Iraqi people love their oppressors or desire their own enslavement. Men and women in every culture need liberty like they need food and water and air. Everywhere that freedom arrives, humanity rejoices; and everywhere that freedom stirs, let tyrants fear.

We have difficult work to do in Iraq. We're bringing order to parts of that country that remain dangerous. We're pursuing and finding leaders of the old regime, who will be held to account for their crimes. We've begun the search for hidden chemical and biological weapons and already know of hundreds of sites that will be investigated. We're helping to rebuild Iraq, where the dictator built palaces for himself, instead of hospitals and schools. And we will stand with the new leaders of Iraq as they establish a government of, by, and for the Iraqi people.

The transition from dictatorship to democracy will take time, but it is worth every effort. Our coalition will stay until our work is done. Then we will leave, and we will leave behind a free Iraq.

The battle of Iraq is one victory in a war on terror that began on September the 11, 2001—and still goes on. That terrible morning, 19 evil men—the shock troops of a hateful ideology—gave America and the civilized world a glimpse of their ambitions. They imagined, in the words of one terrorist, that September the 11th would be the "beginning of the end of America." By seeking to turn our cities into killing fields, terrorists and their allies believed that they could destroy this nation's resolve, and force our retreat from the world. They have failed.

In the battle of Afghanistan, we destroyed the Taliban, many terrorists, and the camps where they trained. We continue to help the Afghan people lay roads, restore hospitals, and educate all of their children. Yet we also have dangerous work to complete. As I speak, a Special Operations task force, led by the 82nd Airborne, is on the trail of the terrorists and those who seek to undermine the free government of Afghanistan. America and our coalition will finish what we have begun.

From Pakistan to the Philippines to the Horn of Africa, we are hunting down al Qaeda killers. Nineteen months ago, I pledged that the terrorists would not escape the patient justice of the United States. And as of tonight, nearly one-half of al Qaeda's senior operatives have been captured or killed.

The liberation of Iraq is a crucial advance in the campaign against terror. We've removed an ally of al Qaeda, and cut off a source of terrorist funding. And this much is certain: No terrorist network will gain weapons of mass destruction from the Iraqi regime, because the regime is no more.

In these 19 months that changed the world, our actions have been focused and deliberate and proportionate to the offense. We have not forgotten the victims of September the 11th—the last phone calls, the cold murder of children, the searches in the rubble. With those attacks, the terrorists and their supporters declared war on the United States. And war is what they got.

Our war against terror is proceeding according to principles that I have made clear to all: Any person involved in committing or planning terrorist attacks against the American people becomes an enemy of this country, and a target of American justice.

Any person, organization, or government that supports, protects, or harbors terrorists is complicit in the murder of the innocent, and equally guilty of terrorist crimes.

Any outlaw regime that has ties to terrorist groups and seeks or possesses weapons of mass destruction is a grave danger to the civilized world—and will be confronted.

And anyone in the world, including the Arab world, who works and sacrifices for freedom has a loyal friend in the United States of America.

Our commitment to liberty is America's tradition—declared at our founding; affirmed in Franklin Roosevelt's Four Freedoms; asserted in the Truman Doctrine and in Ronald Reagan's challenge to an evil empire. We are committed to freedom in Afghanistan, in Iraq, and in a peaceful Palestine. The advance of freedom is the surest strategy to undermine the appeal of terror in the world. Where freedom takes hold, hatred gives way to hope. When freedom takes hold, men and women turn to the peaceful pursuit of a better life. American values and American interests lead in the same direction: We stand for human liberty.

The United States upholds these principles of security and freedom in many ways—with all the tools of diplomacy, law enforcement, intelligence, and finance. We're working with a broad coalition of nations that understand the threat and our shared responsibility to meet it. The use of force has been—and remains—our last resort. Yet all can know, friend and foe alike, that our nation has a mission: We will answer threats to our security, and we will defend the peace.

Our mission continues. Al Qaeda is wounded, not destroyed. The scattered cells of the terrorist network still operate in many nations, and we know from daily intelligence that they continue to plot against free people. The proliferation of deadly weapons remains a serious danger. The enemies of freedom are not idle, and neither are we. Our government has taken unprecedented measures to defend the homeland. And we will continue to hunt down the enemy before he can strike.

The war on terror is not over; yet it is not endless. We do not know the day of final victory, but we have seen the turning of the tide. No act of the terrorists will change our purpose, or weaken our resolve, or alter their fate. Their cause is lost. Free nations will press on to victory.

Other nations in history have fought in foreign lands and remained to occupy and exploit. Americans, following a battle, want nothing more than to return home. And that is your direction tonight. After service in the Afghan—and Iraqi theaters of war—after 100,000 miles, on the longest carrier deployment in recent history, you are homeward bound. Some of you will see new family members for the first time— 150 babies were born while their fathers were on the *Lincoln*. Your families are proud of you, and your nation will welcome you.

We are mindful, as well, that some good men and women are not making the journey home. One of those who fell, Corporal Jason Mileo, spoke to his parents five days before his death. Jason's father said, "He called us from the center of Baghdad, not to brag, but to tell us he loved us. Our son was a soldier."

Every name, every life is a loss to our military, to our nation, and to the loved ones who grieve. There's no homecoming for these families. Yet we pray, in God's time, their reunion will come.

Those we lost were last seen on duty. Their final act on this Earth was to fight a great evil and bring liberty to others. All of you—all in this generation of our military—have taken up the highest calling of history. You're defending your country, and protecting the innocent from harm. And wherever you go, you carry a message of hope—a message that is ancient and ever new. In the words of the prophet Isaiah, "To the captives, 'come out,'—and to those in darkness, 'be free.'"

Thank you for serving our country and our cause. May God bless you all, and may God continue to bless America.

George W. Bush, remarks aboard the USS *Abraham Lincoln*, May 1, 2003.

Document 10: Progress on the Economy

Although the centerpiece of Bush's 2004 State of the Union Address was his defense of the war against terrorism, the president also defended his policies on the economy and education.

In the last three years, adversity has revealed the fundamental strengths of the American economy. We have come through recession, and terrorist attack, and corporate scandals, and the uncertainties of war. And because you [Congress] acted to stimulate our economy with tax relief, this economy is strong, and growing stronger.

You have doubled the child tax credit from $500 to $1,000, reduced the marriage penalty, begun to phase out the death tax, reduced taxes on capital gains and stock dividends, cut taxes on small businesses, and you have lowered taxes for every American who pays income taxes.

Americans took those dollars and put them to work, driving this economy forward. The pace of economic growth in the third quarter of 2003 was the fastest in nearly 20 years; new home construction, the highest in almost 20 years; home ownership rates, the highest ever. Manufacturing activity is increasing. Inflation is low. Interest rates are low. Exports are growing. Productivity is high, and jobs are on the rise.

These numbers confirm that the American people are using their money far better than government would have—and you were right to return it.

America's growing economy is also a changing economy. As technology transforms the way almost every job is done, America becomes more productive, and workers need new skills. Much of our job growth will be found in high-skilled fields like health care and bio-technology. So we must respond by helping more Americans gain the skills to find good jobs in our new economy.

All skills begin with the basics of reading and math, which are supposed to be learned in the early grades of our schools. Yet for too long, for too many children, those skills were never mastered. By passing the No Child Left Behind Act, you have made the expectation of literacy the law of our country. We're providing more funding for our schools—a 36-percent increase since 2001. We're requiring higher standards. We are regularly testing every child on the fundamentals. We are reporting results to parents, and making sure they have better options when schools are not performing. We are making progress toward excellence for every child in America.

But the status quo always has defenders. Some want to undermine the No Child Left Behind Act by weakening standards and accountability. Yet the results we require are really a matter of common sense: We expect third graders to read and do math at the third grade level—and that's not asking too much. Testing is the only way to identify and help students who are falling behind. This nation will not go back to the days of simply shuffling children along from grade to grade without them learning the basics. I refuse to give up on any child—and the No Child Left Behind Act is opening the door of opportunity to all of America's children.

At the same time, we must ensure that older students and adults can gain the skills they need to find work now. Many of the fastest growing occupations require strong math and science preparation, and training beyond the high school level. So tonight, I propose a series of measures called Jobs for the 21st Century. This program will provide extra help to middle and high school students who fall behind in reading and math, expand advanced placement programs in low-income schools, invite math and science professionals from the private sector to teach part-time in our high schools. I propose larger Pell grants for students who prepare for college with demanding courses in high school. I propose increasing our support for America's fine community colleges, so they can—I do so, so they can train workers for industries that are creating the most new jobs. By all these actions, we'll help more and more Americans to join in the growing prosperity of our country. Job training is important, and so is job creation.

We must continue to pursue an aggressive, pro-growth economic agenda. Congress has some unfinished business on the issue of taxes. The tax reductions you passed are set to expire. Unless you act—unless you act—unless you act, the unfair tax on marriage will go back up. Unless you act, millions of families will be charged $300 more in federal taxes for every child. Unless you act, small businesses will pay higher taxes. Unless you act, the death tax will eventually come back to life. Unless you act, Americans face a tax increase. What Congress has given, the Congress should not take away. For the sake of job growth, the tax cuts you passed should be permanent.

Our agenda for jobs and growth must help small business owners and employees with relief from needless federal regulation, and protect them from junk and frivolous lawsuits.

Consumers and businesses need reliable supplies of energy to make our economy run—so I urge you to pass legislation to modernize our electricity system, promote conservation, and make America less dependent on foreign sources of energy.

My administration is promoting free and fair trade to open up new markets for America's entrepreneurs and manufacturers and farmers—to create jobs for American workers. Younger workers should have the opportunity to build a nest egg by saving part of their Social Security taxes in a personal retirement account. We should make the Social Security system a source of ownership for the American people. And we should limit the burden of government on this economy by acting as good stewards of taxpayers' dollars.

George W. Bush, State of the Union Address, January 20, 2004.

Document 11: Staying the Course in Iraq

Although Bush declared an end to major combat in May 2003, violence in Iraq continued and became especially heavy in the spring of 2004. In response, Bush held a prime-time press conference to assert a U.S. commitment to peace, stability, and a sovereign democratic government in Iraq.

This has been tough weeks in [Iraq]. Coalition forces have encountered serious violence in some areas of Iraq. Our military commanders report that this violence is being instigated by three groups: Some remnants of Saddam Hussein's regime, along with Islamic militants have attacked coalition forces in the city of Fallujah. Terrorists from other countries have infiltrated Iraq to incite and organize attacks. In the south of Iraq, coalition forces face riots and attacks that are being incited by a radical cleric named al-Sadr. He has assembled some of his supporters into an illegal militia, and publicly supported the terrorist groups, Hamas and Hezbollah. Al-Sadr's methods of violence and intimidation are widely repudiated by other Iraqi Shia. He's been indicted by Iraqi authorities for the murder of a prominent Shia cleric.

Although these instigations of violence come from different factions, they share common goals. They want to run us out of Iraq and destroy the democratic hopes of the Iraqi people. The violence we have seen is a power grab by these extreme and ruthless elements.

It's not a civil war; it's not a popular uprising. Most of Iraq is relatively stable. Most Iraqis, by far, reject violence and oppose dictatorship. In forums where Iraqis have met to discuss their political future, and in all the proceedings of the Iraqi Governing Council, Iraqis have expressed clear commitments. They want strong protections for individual rights; they want their independence; and they want their freedom.

America's commitment to freedom in Iraq is consistent with our ideals, and required by our interests. Iraq will either be a peaceful, democratic country, or it will again be a source of violence, a haven for terror, and a threat to America and to the world. By helping to secure a free Iraq, Americans serving in that country are protecting their fellow citizens. Our nation is grateful to them all, and to their families that face hardship and long separation.

This weekend, at a Fort Hood hospital, I presented a Purple Heart to some of our wounded; had the honor of thanking them on behalf of all Americans. Other men and women have paid an even greater cost. Our nation honors the memory of those who have been killed, and we pray that their families will find God's comfort in the midst of their grief. As I have said to those who have lost loved ones, we will finish the work of the fallen.

America's armed forces are performing brilliantly, with all the skill and honor we expect of them. We're constantly reviewing their needs. Troop strength, now and in the future, is determined by the situation on the ground. If additional forces are needed, I will send them. If additional resources are needed, we will provide them. The people of our country are united behind our men and women in uniform, and this government will do all that is necessary to assure the success of their historic mission.

One central commitment of that mission is the transfer of sovereignty back to the Iraqi people. We have set a deadline of June 30th. It is important that we meet that deadline. As a proud and independent people, Iraqis do not support an indefinite occupation—and neither does America. We're not an imperial power, as nations such as Japan and Germany can attest. We are a liberating power, as nations in Europe and Asia can attest, as well. America's objective in Iraq is limited, and it is firm: We seek an independent, free and secure Iraq.

Were the coalition to step back from the June 30th pledge, many Iraqis would question our intentions and feel their hopes betrayed. And those in Iraq who trade in hatred and conspiracy theories would find a larger audience and gain a stronger hand. We will not step back from our pledge. On June 30th, Iraqi sovereignty will be placed in Iraqi hands.

Sovereignty involves more than a date and a ceremony. It requires Iraqis to assume responsibility for their own future. Iraqi authorities are now confronting the security challenge of the last several weeks. In Fallujah, coalition forces have suspended offensive operations, allowing members of the Iraqi Governing Council and local leaders to work on the restoration of central authority in that city. These leaders are communicating with the insurgents to ensure an orderly turnover of that city to Iraqi forces, so that the resumption of military action does not become necessary. They're also insisting that those who killed and mutilated four American contract workers be handed over for trial and punishment. In addition, members of the Governing Council are seeking to resolve the situation in the south. Al-Sadr must answer the charges against him and disband his illegal militia.

Our coalition is standing with responsible Iraqi leaders as they establish growing authority in their country. The transition to sovereignty requires that we demonstrate confidence in Iraqis, and we have that confidence. Many Iraqi leaders are showing great personal courage, and their example will bring out the same quality in others. The transition to sovereignty also requires an atmosphere of security, and our coalition is working to provide that security. We will continue taking the greatest care to prevent harm to innocent civilians; yet we will not permit the spread of chaos and violence. I have directed our military commanders to make every preparation to use decisive force, if necessary, to maintain order and to protect our troops.

The nation of Iraq is moving toward self-rule, and Iraqis and Americans will see evidence in the months to come. On June 30th, when the flag of free Iraq is raised, Iraqi officials will assume full responsibility for the ministries of government. On that day, the transitional administrative law, including a bill of rights that is unprecedented in the Arab world, will take full effect.

The United States, and all the nations of our coalition, will establish normal diplomatic relations with the Iraqi government. An American embassy will open, and an American ambassador will be posted.

According to the schedule already approved by the Governing Council, Iraq will hold elections for a national assembly no later than next January. That assembly will draft a new, permanent constitution which will be presented to the Iraqi people in a national referendum held in October of next year. Iraqis will then elect a permanent government by December 15, 2005—an event that will mark the completion of Iraq's transition from dictatorship to freedom.

Other nations and international institutions are stepping up to their responsibilities in building a free and secure Iraq. We're working closely with the United Nations envoy, Lakhdar Brahimi, and with Iraqis to determine the exact form of the government that will receive sovereignty on June 30th. The United Nations election assistance team, headed by Karina Parelli (phonetic), is in Iraq, developing plans for next January's election. NATO is providing support for the Polish-led multinational division in Iraq. And 17 of NATO's 26 members are contributing forces to maintain security.

Secretary of State Powell and Secretary of State Rumsfeld, and a number of NATO defense and foreign ministers are exploring a more formal role for NATO, such as turning the Polish-led division into a NATO operation, and giving NATO specific responsibilities for border control.

Iraqi's neighbors also have responsibilities to make their region more stable. So I am sending Deputy Secretary of State Armitage to the Middle East to discuss with these nations our common interest in a free and independent Iraq, and how they can help achieve this goal.

As we've made clear all along, our commitment to the success and security of Iraq will not end on June 30th. On July 1st, and beyond, our reconstruction assistance will continue, and our military commitment will continue. Having helped Iraqis establish a new government, coalition military forces will help Iraqis to protect their government from external aggression and internal subversion.

The success of free government in Iraq is vital for many reasons. A free Iraq is vital because 25 million Iraqis have as much right to live in freedom as we do. A free Iraq will stand as an example to reformers across the Middle East. A free Iraq will show that America is on the side of Muslims who wish to live in peace, as we have already shown in Kuwait and Kosovo, Bosnia and Afghanistan. A free Iraq will confirm to a watching world that America's word, once given, can be relied upon, even in the toughest times.

Above all, the defeat of violence and terror in Iraq is vital to the defeat of violence and terror elsewhere; and vital, therefore, to the safety of the American people. Now is the time, and Iraq is the place, in which the enemies of the civilized world are testing the will of the civilized world. We must not waver.

The violence we are seeing in Iraq is familiar. The terrorist who takes hostages, or plants a roadside bomb near Baghdad is serving the same ideology of murder that kills innocent people on trains in Madrid, and murders children on buses in Jerusalem, and blows up a nightclub in Bali, and cuts the throat of a young reporter for being a Jew.

We've seen the same ideology of murder in the killing of 241 Marines in Beirut, the first attack on the World Trade Center, in the destruction of two embassies in Africa, in the attack on the USS *Cole*, and in the merciless horror inflicted upon thousands of innocent men and women and children on September the 11th, 2001.

None of these acts is the work of a religion; all are the work of a fanatical, political ideology. The servants of this ideology seek tyranny in the Middle East and beyond. They seek to oppress and persecute women. They seek the death of Jews and Christians, and every Muslim who desires peace over theocratic terror. They seek to intimidate America into panic and retreat, and to set free nations against each other. And they seek weapons of mass destruction, to blackmail and murder on a massive scale.

Over the last several decades, we've seen that any concession or retreat on our part will only embolden this enemy and invite more bloodshed. And the enemy has seen, over the last 31 months, that we will no longer live in denial or seek to appease them. For the first time, the civilized world has provided a concerted response to the ideology of terror—a series of powerful, effective blows.

The terrorists have lost the shelter of the Taliban and the training camps in Afghanistan. They've lost safe havens in Pakistan. They lost an ally in Baghdad. And Libya has turned its back on terror. They've lost many leaders in an unrelenting international manhunt. And perhaps most frightening to these men and their movement, the terrorists are seeing the advance of freedom and reform in the greater Middle East.

A desperate enemy is also a dangerous enemy, and our work may become more difficult before it is finished. No one can predict all the hazards that lie ahead, or the costs they will bring. Yet, in this conflict, there is no safe alternative to resolute action. The consequences of failure in Iraq would be unthinkable. Every friend of America and Iraq would be betrayed to prison and murder as a new tyranny arose. Every enemy of America and the world would celebrate, proclaiming our weakness and decadence, and using that victory to recruit a new generation of killers.

We will succeed in Iraq. We're carrying out a decision that has already been made and will not change: Iraq will be a free, independent country, and America and the Middle East will be safer because of it. Our coalition has the means and the will to prevail. We serve the cause of liberty, and that is, always and everywhere, a cause worth serving.

George W. Bush, prime-time press conference, April 13, 2004.

CHRONOLOGY

JULY 6, 1946
George Walker Bush is born to Barbara Pierce Bush and George Herbert Walker Bush in New Haven, Connecticut.

1948
George H.W. Bush moves the family to Odessa, Texas, when he becomes involved in the oil business.

1953
Robin Bush, George junior's sister, dies of leukemia.

1961
Like his father, George W. Bush completes high school at the prestigious Phillips Academy in Andover, Massachusetts.

1964
Following his father's footsteps, Bush enrolls at Yale University; he joins Yale's secretive Skull and Bones Society.

1968
Bush graduates from Yale; he joins the Texas Air National Guard and is trained as a fighter pilot; Bush serves until 1973.

1975
Bush receives a master of business administration from Harvard University and begins work in the oil industry in Midland, Texas.

1977
Bush marries Laura Welch on November 5 in Midland, Texas.

1978
Bush campaigns unsuccessfully as the Republican candidate for a seat in the U.S. House of Representatives but manages to gain 47 percent of the vote in a district that had never elected a Republican.

1980
Ronald Reagan is elected president of the United States; George H.W. Bush becomes vice president.

1981
Twin girls are born to the Bushes; they are named Barbara and Jenna after their grandmothers.

1983
Bush becomes chief executive officer for Spectrum 7, an energy company.

1986
After a drinking binge to celebrate his fortieth birthday, Bush stops using alcohol and becomes a devout Christian.

1988
Bush works on his father's successful presidential campaign.

1989
George H.W. Bush is sworn in as the forty-first president of the United States; George W. Bush and a group of investors purchase the Texas Rangers baseball team; Bush is the managing partner of the team until 1994.

1994
Bush defeats the popular incumbent Ann Richards to become governor of Texas; once in office, Bush becomes noted for his ability to craft policies that garner bipartisan support.

1995
Bush declares an "emergency" over tort laws in Texas and is able to convince the legislature to enact wide-ranging tort reform; he also proposes, and the Texas legislature approves, a series of initiatives aimed at reducing juvenile crime through increased penalties and new juvenile detention centers.

1997
Health maintenance organization (HMO) reform designed to give patients more choice is enacted in Texas.

1998
Bush is reelected by a wide margin and becomes the first governor of Texas in the modern era to be reelected to consecutive four-year terms.

2000
In a bitterly contested election, Bush wins with 271 electoral votes to his opponent's, incumbent vice president Al Gore, 266 electoral votes; Bush loses the popular vote by five hundred thousand votes and the election is ultimately decided by a controversial recount in Florida.

JANUARY 2001
On January 20 Bush is inaugurated as the forty-third president of the United States.

APRIL 2001
On April 1 a U.S. Navy spy plane collides with a Chinese fighter and is forced to land in China; the crisis is resolved peacefully after the Chinese release the American crew.

MAY 17, 2001
Bush announces a sweeping energy plan that includes a controversial proposal to drill for oil in the Alaska National Wildlife Refuge. Later that month Senator Jim Jeffords of Vermont leaves the Republican Party and becomes an independent, which gives control of the Senate to the Democratic Party.

MAY 26, 2001
Congress approves the first in a series of multiple tax cuts proposed by Bush during his first term.

SEPTEMBER 11, 2001
Al Qaeda terrorists launch attacks that destroy the twin towers of the World Trade Center in New York and damage the Pentagon; a fourth hijacked plane crashes in Pennsylvania after passengers attack the hijackers; the nation goes on full military alert and Bush pledges to make "no distinction" between the terrorists and regimes, such as the Taliban of Afghanistan, that support them;

Bush will later propose the creation of an office of homeland security in response to the attack.

OCTOBER 7, 2001
Coalition forces led by the United States and Great Britain attack the Taliban and al Qaeda in Afghanistan; by December the Taliban regime is removed from power.

DECEMBER 13, 2001
Bush announces that the United States will unilaterally withdraw from the 1972 Anti-Ballistic Missile (ABM) Treaty.

JANUARY 8, 2002
Bush signs the No Child Left Behind Act, a broad educational package designed to improve student performance through accountability standards, including extensive use of standardized testing.

MARCH 27, 2002
Bush signs into law the McCain-Feingold Campaign Reform Act in order to limit the spending of special interest groups in federal elections.

JUNE 2002
Bush launches a diplomatic initiative known as the "Roadmap for Peace" in an attempt to settle the Palestinian-Israeli conflict.

SEPTEMBER 2002
Bush publishes a new national security strategy that formalizes the Bush Doctrine, which holds that the United States must attack nations that pose a potential threat to U.S. security.

NOVEMBER 2002
Counter to historical trends the Republicans gain congressional seats in the midterm elections and regain control of the Senate.

JANUARY 28, 2003
In his State of the Union speech, Bush announces that the United States will use force against Iraqi dictator Saddam Hussein if he does not voluntarily disarm; throughout the winter the United

States endeavors unsuccessfully to gain UN approval for an invasion of Iraq; a diplomatic crisis ensues between the United States and allies such as France and Germany, which oppose the war.

FEBRUARY 1, 2003
The space shuttle *Columbia* breaks apart while returning to the earth.

MARCH 2003
On March 19 U.S.-led forces attack Iraq, within a month, coalition troops have captured Baghdad.

MAY 1, 2003
Bush declares an official end to major combat in Iraq.

MAY 28, 2003
In spite of the growing federal deficit, Bush secures the third-largest tax cut in American history ($330 billion) in an effort to stimulate the national economy.

NOVEMBER 27, 2003
Under heavy security, Bush travels to Iraq to have Thanksgiving dinner with American troops.

DECEMBER 8, 2003
Bush signs a $400 billion Medicare reform bill, which offers prescription drug benefits for seniors for the first time.

DECEMBER 14, 2003
Saddam Hussein is captured by U.S. troops in Iraq.

JANUARY 14, 2004
Bush calls for a renewed space program with goals of returning astronauts to the moon by 2015 and an eventual manned-mission to Mars.

APRIL 13, 2004
As violence in Iraq escalated, leading to increased U.S. casualties, Bush held a prime-time press conference to state America's commitment to overseeing Iraq's transfer to a stable, democratic regime.

FOR FURTHER RESEARCH

BIOGRAPHY

ERIC ALTERMAN AND MARK J. GREEN, *The Book on Bush: How George W. (Mis)leads America.* New York: Viking, 2004.

IVO H. DAALDER AND JAMES M. LINDSAY, *America Unbound: The Bush Revolution in Foreign Policy.* Washington, DC: Brookings Institution Press, 2003.

DAVID FRUM, *The Right Man: The Surprise Presidency of George W. Bush.* New York: Random House, 2003.

J.H. HATFIELD, *Fortunate Son: George W. Bush and the Making of an American President.* Brooklyn, NY: Soft Skull, 2002.

BILL MINUTAGLIO, *First Son: George W. Bush and the Bush Family Dynasty.* New York: Three Rivers, 2001.

JAMES MOORE AND WAYNE SLATER, *Bush's Brain: How Karl Rove Made George W. Bush Presidential.* New York: John Wiley & Sons, 2003.

KEVIN PHILLIPS, *American Dynasty: Aristocracy, Fortune, and the Politics of Deceit in the House of Bush.* New York: Viking, 2004.

RON SUSKIND, *The Price of Loyalty: George W. Bush, the White House, and the Education of Paul O'Neill.* New York: Simon & Schuster, 2004.

BOB WOODWARD, *Bush at War.* New York: Simon & Schuster, 2002.

ANALYSIS OF THE BUSH PRESIDENCY

COLIN CAMPBELL AND BERT A. ROCKMAN, EDS., *The George Bush Presidency: First Appraisals.* Chatham, NJ: Chatham House, 2003.

FRED I. GREENSTEIN, ED., *The George W. Bush Presidency: An Early Assessment.* Baltimore: Johns Hopkins University Press, 2003.

GARY L. GREGG II AND MARK J. ROZELL, EDS., *Considering the Bush Presidency.* New York: Oxford University Press, 2004.

BRYAN HILLIARD, TOM LANSFORD, AND ROBERT P. WATSON, EDS., *George W. Bush: Evaluating the President at Midterm.* Albany, NY: SUNY Press, 2004.

GARY C. JACOBSON AND SAMUEL KERNELL, *The Logic of American Politics in Wartime: Lessons from the Bush Administration.* Washington, DC: CQ Press, 2004.

KEVIN J. MCMAHON, DAVID M. RANKIN, AND JON KRAUS, EDS., *Transformed by Crisis: The Presidency of George W. Bush and American Politics.* New York: Palgrave Macmillan, 2004.

BOOKS BY BUSH

GEORGE W. BUSH, *A Charge to Keep: My Journey to the White House.* Madison, WI: Turtleback, 2001.

GEORGE W. BUSH, *We Will Prevail: President George W. Bush on War, Terrorism, and Freedom.* Ed. Peggy Noonan. New York: Continuum, 2003.

WEB SITES

AMERICAN PRESIDENTS: LIFE PORTRAITS, www.americanpresidents. org. Based on the popular C-SPAN series of the same name, this site contains facts on Bush, his inaugural address, and links to other resources and related sites. Visitors to the site may view segments of the popular televised series.

ON THE ISSUES, www.issues2000.org. The site's claim is "every political leader on every issue," which is not far from the truth. Visitors to this site will find a comprehensive selection of leaders with information on their political record. The Bush record is examined for international issues (from foreign policy to trade), domestic issues (from the environment to gun control), economic issues (from taxes to technology), and social issues (from abortion to education).

OPEN SECRETS, www.opensecrets.org/2000/elect/index/P0000335. htm. This is a helpful resource for advocates of political reform. The site contains information many politicians might not want the public to see, such as records on their campaign fund-raising, donations, and expenditures, including money donated from individuals and political action committees (PACs). It also examines the Bush cabinet, Bush's first one hundred days in office, and even his days as governor of Texas.

INDEX

of, 59–60
staff of, vs. staff of George W. Bush,
    177–78
transition into presidency by, 168–69
coal industry, 154
Colvin, Joe, 156
Connaughton, James L., 136
corporate community
    energy/environmental policy and,
        140–41, 152
    energy industry interests of, 152–55
    is pleased with Bush administration, 57
Corrie, Rachel, 79–80
Council on Environmental Quality
    (CEQ), 134
Creppy, Michael, 86

Daalder, Ivo H., 43
Daschle, Thomas, 155, 195
defense spending. *See* military spending
deficit, the
    basic nature of, 109–10
    is harmless, 111–12
    putting, into perspective, 94
    was unavoidable, 108–109
Delta Kappa Epsilon, 12
Department of Homeland Security
    (DHS), 25, 62, 76
    see also national security
DeWine, Mike, 70
Dingell, John, 156–58
Dinosaur National Monument, 137
Dole, Elizabeth, 192
domestic policy. *See* economy, the;
    education; environmental policy
Draft Enforcement Plan, 39

Eagleburger, Lawrence, 46
Economist (magazine), 118
economy, the
    aftereffects of Bush's strategy on,
        100–101
    Bush's spending strategy and, 104–105
    entitlement-reform agenda in, 98
    health care costs and, 96–98
    national security spending and, 62–63
    policy mistakes for, 103–104
    revenue losses for government and,
        102–103
    revolution in, 98–99
    see also deficit, the; military spending;
        tax cuts
Edison Electric Institute, 153
education, 22
    annual testing in, 115

bipartisan consensus on, 116–17
Clinton's reforms in, 115–16
see also No Child Left Behind Act
Education Trust, 128
elections
    1978, 13
    1992, 15
    1994, 16
    1998, 17
    2000, 17–18, 165–66
    2002 midterm, 20–21
        downplaying victory in, 188–89
        George W. Bush hears results of,
            186–87
        results for Democrats vs. Republicans
            in, 189–91
        strategy of Bush team for, 188, 191–92,
            193
        war on terror helped Republican
            victory in, 190
    see also fundraising
electric utility industry, 153–54
Elementary and Secondary Education Act
    (ESEA), 115–16, 125
    see also No Child Left Behind Act
El Paso Corporation, 153
Endangered Species Act, 138
Enron, 161
environmental policy, 22–23
    Clinton policy on, 135–36
    corporate interests and, 140–41, 152–55,
        159–61
    energy development prioritized under,
        135, 136–37, 139–40
    giving credit to Bush for, 146–48
    on greenhouse gas reductions, 141–42
    habit and species protection under, 146
    increase in energy development and,
        142–43
    on mercury emissions, 144–45
    national parks are jeopardized under,
        137–38
    on pollution control, 143–44
    preservation of federal lands and,
        134–35
    public opposition to, 138–39, 140
    rewriting environmental protection
        statutes under, 138
    spent nuclear fuel and, 155–56
    task force for, 151–52
        secrecy of, 156–59, 162
    thinning of national forests under,
        145–46
Environmental Protection Agency (EPA),
    139, 154

support for George W. Bush and, 188
without UN backing, 54
weapons inspections and, 26
Islamic extremism, 74
Israel, 63–64
Italy, 26–27

Jacobson, Gary C., 190
Japan, 26–27
Jeffords, James, 158, 183
Jones, Charles O., 169
Judicial Watch, 159, 162

Kennedy, Edward M., 117, 119, 124
Kernell, Samuel, 190
Kissinger, Henry, 46
Koch Industries, 153
Kovacs, William T., 141
Kress, Sandy, 119, 121
Kriz, Margaret, 133
Kulongoski, Ted, 130

Lay, Kenneth, 161
League of Conservation Voters, 141
Leavitt, Mike, 137
Ledlord, Angela, 144
legislation
    on the environment, 138
    see also No Child Left Behind Act; USA
        PATRIOT Act
Lewis, Charles, 149
Libby, I. Lewis, 182
Lieberman, Joseph I., 116
Lindsay, James M., 43
Lundquist, Andrew, 157

Maltese, John Anthony, 165
Matalin, Mary, 182
Mathis, William J., 129
Matz, Mike, 143
media
    cover-up by, of September 11 security
        failure, 59–60
    ignored security-protectors, 60–61
    positive portrayal of Bush in, 56–57
    secrecy between Bush administration
        and, 184
    on terrorist threats, 61
Medicare, 96, 104
Mehlman, Ken, 181, 194
Mercado, Marta, 170–71
Mexico, 41, 53–54
military
    Bush's concerns on, 37–38
    post–September 11 projects and funding

for, 61–62
military spending, 22
    domestic appropriations vs., 105–106
    September 11 and, 94–95
military tribunals, 76, 77
Miller, George, 116, 118–19, 124
Miller, Zell, 194–95
Mineta, Norman, 172
Minnesota, 129–30
missile defense system, 22
Moquith Mountain and Parunuweap
    Canyon, 134
Morris, Dick, 180

Naatz, Daniel T., 136
Nadler, Richard, 93
National Assessment of Educational
    Progress (NAEP), 120, 125
National Conference of State Legislatures
    (NCSL), 131–32
National Crime Information Center
    database, 88
National Energy Policy Development
    Group, 152
National Environmental Policy Act
    (NEPA), 142–43
National Missile Defense (NMD), 62
national security
    election of 2000 and, 194–95
    ethnic/racial profiling and, 78–80, 87–88
    evading blame for failure of, 59–60
    failure in, 55–56
        before September 11, 11, 57, 58
        media ignoring, 56–57
    financial costs of, 101
    funding for, 62–63
    has not improved our safety, 70–71
    impact of, on immigration policy,
        84–86, 88–91
    need for self-policing and, 76–77
    new surveillance techniques for, 80–81
    reasons for tightening, 74–76
    spending money on military vs., 61–62
    state funding for, 106–107
    trading civil liberties for, 68–70
    wasting money on, 62–63
    weapons of mass destruction and, 25–26
Natural Resources Defense Council
    (NRDC), 159–60
New Hampshire, 129–30
New York Times (newspaper), 34
No Child Left Behind Act
    backlash against, by states, 129–30
    bipartisan negotiations for, 118–19
    complicated requirements for, 125–26

fearmongering following, 61–63
financial costs of, 94–95
impact of
    on education bill, 119
    on George W. Bush, 31–32
    on George W. Bush's presidency,
        174–75
    on immigration policy, 83–84, 89–90
    international collegiality and, 39–41
    on U.S. foreign policy, 10
lack of evidence linking Iraq to, 27
security failure leading, 57–58
security-protectors following, 60–61
see also national security; war on terror
Sharif, Omar Khan, 80
Sharon, Ariel, 63–64
Shell Oil Company, 153
Shreve, David, 132
Sierra Club, 141, 162
Social Security privatization, 97–98
Southern Methodist University, 13
Spain, 26–27
Spelling, Margaret, 178
state education requirements, 120–22,
    126–27, 131
Stevens, Ted, 150
Student and Exchange Visitor Information
    System, 90
Suro, Roberto, 82

Taliban prisoners, 64
tax cuts, 21–22, 95–96, 101–102
Tenpas, Kathryn Dunn, 176
terrorism
    instilling fears about, 60–63
    manufacturing, 63–64
    racial profiling and, 78–80
    reporting suspicions on, 75–76
    see also war on terror
Terrorist Information and Prevention
    System (TIPS), 75–76
Texas Air National Guard, 13
Texas Rangers professional baseball team,
    14–16
Texas Utilities (TXU), 153, 154
Thomas, Norman C., 165
tort reforms, 16–17
transition into office
    choosing staff during
        Bush's, compared with predecessors',
            176–79
        expansion of staff positions and,
            181–83
        good cabinet choices and, 170–72
        minority appointments and, 178

election presented challenges to, 18–20,
    165–66
funding and office space for, 166–67
of George W. Bush, vs. Clinton, 168–69
good start to, 169–72
missteps in, 183
obstacles to planning for, 167–68

United Kingdom, 26–27
United Nations (UN)
    backing for Iraq war from
        disagreements over receiving, 45, 46
        military operations initiating without,
            54
    George H.W. Bush and, 12
    Security Council resolutions of, 26, 27,
        47–49, 50–51
    U.S. going to, under false pretenses,
        49–50
    World Conference against Racism,
        Xenophobia, and Related Prejudice, 39
University of Texas, 13
UN Resolution 1441, 50, 51
USA PATRIOT Act (2001), 68–69, 73, 77
U.S. Justice Department, 86–87, 90
U.S. Supreme Court, 18
Utah, 134

Vietnam War, 13, 63

Walker, David, 157, 158
war on terror
    civil liberties vs., 25
    as focus of Bush's presidency, 37
    helped Republican victory in 2000
        election, 190
    justification for, 64–65
    see also Iraq war
Waxman, Henry, 156–58, 161
weapons inspections
    Blix on, 52–53
    decision for UN, 47–48
    Iraq's failure to comply with, 51–52
    rationale for war and, 26
    UN resolutions and, 47–51
weapons of mass destruction
    Bush's credibility and, 27
    Iraq's destruction of, 53
    national security and, 25–26
Whitman, Christine Todd, 139, 140, 172
World Trade Center bombing, 89

Yale University, 12
Yucca Mountain, 155

About the Editors

Tom Lansford, PhD, is associate professor of political science at the University of Southern Mississippi and a fellow with the Frank Maria Center for International Politics and Ethics. He is the author or editor of over a dozen books, including, *All for One: Terrorism, NATO, and the United States* (2002), and has published many dozens of scholarly articles, chapters, and essays.

Robert P. Watson, PhD, is associate professor of political science at Florida Atlantic University and editor of the journal *White House Studies*. He is the author or editor of over twenty books, including *The Presidents' Wives: Reassessing the Office of First Lady* (2000), and has published more than one hundred scholarly articles, chapters, and essays.

Both Lansford and Watson have convened national conferences on the presidency and serve on the boards of numerous professional associations and journals. The two have written or edited several books together, including Greenhaven Press's *Presidents and Their Decisions: Theodore Roosevelt* and *Presidents and Their Decisions: John F. Kennedy.*